D1220914

WITHDRAWN

Favorite Fairy Tales
Told Around the World

Favorite Fairy Tales Told Around the World

Retold by Virginia Haviland

Illustrated by S. D. Schindler

LITTLE, BROWN AND COMPANY
BOSTON TORONTO

J398.208
F

ILLUSTRATIONS COPYRIGHT © 1985 BY S. D. SCHINDLER
TEXT COPYRIGHT © 1959, 1961, 1963, 1965, 1966, 1967, 1970, 1971, 1973, 1985 BY VIRGINIA HAVILAND
ALL RIGHTS RESERVED. NO PART OF THIS BOOK MAY BE REPRODUCED IN ANY FORM OR BY ANY ELECTRONIC OR MECHANICAL MEANS INCLUDING INFORMATION STORAGE AND RETRIEVAL SYSTEMS WITHOUT PERMISSION IN WRITING FROM THE PUBLISHER, EXCEPT BY A REVIEWER WHO MAY QUOTE BRIEF PASSAGES IN A REVIEW.

FIRST EDITION

Story acknowledgments begin on page 325.

Library of Congress Cataloging in Publication Data

Haviland, Virginia, 1911–
Favorite fairy tales told around the world.

Summary: A compendium of stories from the author's previous books, with several tales from each of sixteen countries.
1. Fairy tales. [1. Fairy tales. 2. Folklore]
I. Schindler, S. D., ill. II. Title.
PZ8.H295Far 1985 398.2'1 83-7941
ISBN 0-316-35044-3

DECATUR PUBLIC LIBRARY
JAN 15 1986
DECATUR, ILLINOIS

BP

Published simultaneously in Canada
by Little, Brown & Company (Canada) Limited

PRINTED IN THE UNITED STATES OF AMERICA

Contents

Preface

WHEN THE FIRST VOLUMES of *Favorite Fairy Tales* were issued in the late fifties, I never imagined they would lead to the publication of a whole series. But the response from reviewers, librarians, and from children themselves was such that the first three collections of stories from England, France, and Germany were followed by collections from countries all over Europe and as far afield as India and Japan. The well-loved stories, retold in simple language from classic sources, proved their enduring quality to a new generation of readers. The series grew to sixteen volumes over the years – each one illustrated by a different artist and produced for an audience accustomed to excellence in book design. The books were all well received, for which I owe much to my editor's foresight as well as to my experience as a children's librarian. This anthology is culled from the series and brings together two or three stories from each of the original volumes. The stories have been newly typeset and illustrated, and it is my belief that in this international collection they will have as great a future as they have had a past.

V.H.

Czechoslovakia

The Wood Fairy

ONCE UPON A TIME there was a little girl named Betushka. She lived with her mother, a poor widow who had only a tumbledown cottage and two goats. But in spite of this poverty, Betushka was always merry.

From spring to autumn Betushka drove the goats each day to pasture in a birch wood. Every morning her mother put a slice of bread and an empty spindle into her bag. The spindle would hold the flaxen thread she would spin while she watched the goats. She was too poor to own a distaff on which to wind the flax, so she wound it around her head, to carry it thus to the wood.

"Work hard, Betushka," her mother always said, "and fill the spindle before you return home."

Off skipped Betushka, singing along the way. She danced behind the goats into the wood of birch trees and sat down under a tree. With her left hand she pulled fibers from the flax around her head and with her right hand twirled her spindle so that it hummed over the ground. All the time she sang merrily and the goats nibbled the green grass among the trees.

When the sun showed that it was midday, Betushka stopped her spinning. She gave each of the goats a morsel of bread and picked a few strawberries to eat with what remained. After this, she sprang up and danced. The sun shone even more warmly and the birds sang yet more sweetly.

After her dance, Betushka began again to spin busily. At evening when she drove the goats home she was able to hand her mother a spindle full of flaxen thread.

One fine spring day, when Betushka was ready as usual to dance, suddenly there appeared before her a most beautiful maiden. Her white dress floated about her as thin as gossamer, her golden hair flowed to her waist, and a wreath of forest blossoms crowned her head. Betushka was struck silent.

The wood fairy smiled at her and in a sweet voice asked, "Betushka, do you like to dance?"

At this, Betushka lost her fear. "Oh! I could dance all the day long!"

"Come then, let us dance together. I will teach you." She took Betushka and began to dance with her.

Round and round they circled, while sweet music sounded over their heads. The maiden had called upon the birds sitting in the birch trees to accompany them. Nightingales, larks, goldfinches, thrushes, and a clever mockingbird sang such sweet melodies that Betushka's heart filled with delight. She quite forgot her goats and her spinning. On and on she danced, with feet never weary, till evening when the last rosy rays of sunset were disappearing. The music ceased and the maiden vanished as suddenly as she had come.

Betushka looked around. There was her spindle—only half filled with thread. Sadly she put it into her bag and drove the goats from the wood. She did not sing while going down the road this time, but reproached herself for forgetting her duty. She resolved she would not do this again. When she reached home she was so quiet that her mother asked if she were ill.

"No, Mother, I am not ill." But she did not tell her mother about the lovely maiden. She hid the half-filled spindle, promising herself to work twice as hard tomorrow to make up for today.

Early the next morning Betushka again drove the goats to pasture, singing merrily as usual. She entered the wood and began her spinning, intending to do twice her usual stint.

At noon Betushka picked a few strawberries, but she did not dance. To her goats she said, "Today, I dare not dance. Why don't *you* dance, my little goats?"

"Come and dance with me," called a voice. It was the beautiful maiden.

But this time Betushka was afraid, and she was also ashamed. She asked the maiden to leave her alone. "Before sunset, I must finish my spinning," she said.

The maiden answered, "If you will dance with me, someone will help you finish your spinning." With the birds singing beautifully, as before, Betushka could not resist. She and the maiden began to dance, and again they danced till evening.

Now when Betushka looked at her nearly empty spindle,

she burst into tears. But the maiden unwound the flax from Betushka's head, twined it around a slender birch tree, seized the spindle, and began to spin. The spindle hummed over the ground and grew thick with thread. By the time the sun had dropped from sight, all the flax was spun. As the maiden handed the full spindle to Betushka, she said, "Wind it and grumble not. Remember, wind it and grumble not." Then, suddenly, she disappeared.

Betushka, happy now, drove the goats home, singing as she went, and gave her mother the full spindle. Betushka's mother, however, was not pleased with what Betushka had failed to do the day before and asked her about it. Betushka told her that she had danced, but she kept the maiden a secret.

The next day Betushka went still earlier to the birch wood. The goats grazed while she sang and spun, until at noon the beautiful maiden appeared and again seized Betushka by the waist to dance. While the birds sang for them, the two danced on and on, Betushka quite forgetting her spindle and the goats.

When the sun was setting, Betushka looked around. There was the half-filled spindle! But the maiden grasped Betushka's bag, became invisible for a moment, then handed back the bag stuffed with something light. She ordered her not to look into it before reaching home, and with these words she disappeared.

Betushka started home, not daring to look into the bag. But halfway there she was unable to resist peeking, for the bag was so light she feared a trick. She looked into the bag, and began to weep. It was full of dry birch leaves! Angrily, she tossed some of these out of the bag, but suddenly she stopped – she knew they would make good litter for the goats to sleep on.

Now she was almost afraid to go home. There her mother was awaiting her. "What kind of spindle did you bring me yesterday?" she asked. "I wound and I wound, but the spindle remained full. 'Some evil spirit has spun you,' I grumbled, and at that instant the thread vanished from the spindle. Tell me what this means."

Betushka then told her mother about the maiden and their dancing. "That was a wood fairy!" exclaimed her mother, alarmed. "The wood fairies dance at midday and at midnight. If you had been a little boy, you might not have escaped alive. But to little girls the wood fairies often give rich presents." Next she added, "To think that you did not tell me. If I had not grumbled I might have had a room full of thread."

Betushka then thought of her bag and wondered if there might not, after all, be something under those leaves. She lifted out the spindle and the unspun flax. "Look, Mother!" Her mother looked and clapped her hands. Under the spindle the birch leaves had turned to gold!

Betushka told her mother how the wood fairy had directed her not to peep into her bag until she got home, but that she had not obeyed and had thrown out some of the leaves. "'Tis fortunate you did not empty out the whole bagful," said her mother.

The next morning Betushka and her mother went to the wood, to look carefully over the ground where Betushka had thrown out the dry leaves. Only fresh birch leaves lay there, but the gold that Betushka did bring home was enough for a farm with a garden and some cows. She wore beautiful dresses and no longer had to graze the goats. Nothing, however, gave her such delight as she had had dancing with the wood fairy. Often she ran to the birch wood, hoping to see the beautiful maiden, but never again did the wood fairy appear.

The Twelve Months

THERE WAS ONCE a widow who had a daughter named Holena. In the cottage with them lived Holena's stepsister, Marushka. Now Marushka was so pretty and good that the other two disliked her and made her do all the hard work. She had to sweep the rooms, cook, wash, sew, spin and weave, and she had to bring in the hay from the meadow and milk the cow. Holena, who was not pretty, did nothing but dress up in her best clothes and amuse herself with one thing after another.

But Marushka never complained. Patiently she bore the scoldings and bad tempers of the mother and daughter. Holena's ugliness increased, while Marushka became even lovelier to look at. This made the other two more tyrannical and grumpy than ever. At length they determined to get rid of her, for they knew that Holena would have no suitors while Marushka was there to be seen.

One day in the middle of winter Holena said she wanted some violets. "Listen!" she cried to Marushka.

"You must go up on the mountain and find me some violets. And they must be fresh and sweet-scented. Do you hear?"

"But whoever heard of violets blooming in the snow!" cried Marushka.

"You wretched creature! Do you dare to disobey me? Not another word! Off with you, and don't come back without the violets!"

The stepmother added her threats, and the two pushed Marushka out of the cottage and shut the door behind her.

Marushka, weeping, made her way to the mountain. The snow lay deep and there was no trace of any other human being. For a long time she wandered hither and thither, and lost herself in the woods. She became hungry and she shivered with cold and was almost ready to give up when she saw a light in the distance. She climbed toward it, until she had reached the very top of the mountain.

Upon the highest peak she found a large fire burning and twelve men in long white robes sitting around it. Three had white hair, three were not quite so old, three were young and handsome, and the rest still younger. These were the twelve months of the year, and they sat silently looking at the fire, each one on a block of stone. The great January was placed higher than the others. He was older than they, and his hair and beard were white as snow. In his hand he held a wand.

At first Marushka was afraid, but after a while her courage returned. Drawing near, she said, "Good men, may I warm myself at your fire? I am chilled by the winter cold."

The great January raised his head and asked, "What brings you here, my child? What do you seek?"

"I am looking for violets," replied Marushka.

"This is not the season for violets. Do you not see the snow everywhere?"

"Yes," was Marushka's reply, "but my stepmother and my stepsister have ordered me to bring them violets from your mountain. If I return without them, they will kill me. I pray you, good sirs, to tell me where to find them."

The great January arose and went over to one of the youngest of the months. Placing his wand in that month's hand, he said, "Brother March, do you take the highest place."

March obeyed, at the same time waving his wand over the fire. Immediately the flames rose toward the sky. The snow began to melt, the trees and shrubs to bud. The grass became green and between the blades peeped the pale primrose. It was spring, and the meadows turned blue with violets.

"Gather them quickly, Marushka," said March.

Joyfully, Marushka hastened to pick the flowers and soon had a large bouquet. She thanked the months and hastened home. Holena and her mother were amazed at the sight of the flowers and at their fragrance, which filled the house.

"Where did you pick them?" asked Holena.

"Under the trees on the mountain," replied Marushka.

Holena took the flowers, but without thanking Marushka for the trouble she had taken to get them.

The next day Holena called to Marushka again and said, "I long to taste strawberries. Run and fetch me some from the mountain, and see to it that they are sweet and ripe."

"But whoever heard of strawberries ripening in the snow?" said Marushka.

"Hold your tongue! Go after the strawberries and don't come back without them."

Holena's mother also ordered Marushka to gather the berries. They pushed her out of the house and bolted the door behind her.

Unhappily, Marushka made her way to the mountain again and climbed until she came to the fire around which sat the twelve months.

"Good men, may I warm myself at your fire? The winter wind chills me."

The great January raised his head and asked, "Why do you come here? What do you seek?"

"I am looking for strawberries," she replied.

"But we are in the midst of winter. Strawberries do not grow in the snow."

"I know," said Marushka sadly, "but my stepmother and stepsister have ordered me to bring them strawberries. I dare not return without them. Pray, good sirs, tell me where to find them."

The great January arose and went over to the month opposite him and, putting his wand into that month's hand, said, "Brother June, do you take the highest place."

June obeyed, and as he waved his wand over the fire, the flames leaped toward the sky. Instantly the snow melted, the earth became green with grass and the trees with leaves. Birds began to sing and flowers blossomed in the forest. It was summer, and in the sunny glades, star-shaped blooms changed into ripe, red strawberries.

"Gather them quickly," said June.

Joyfully, Marushka thanked the months and, when she had filled her apron, ran happily home. The strawberries greatly surprised Holena and her mother. "Wherever did you find them?" asked Holena, crossly.

"Up on the mountain," replied Marushka.

Holena gave a few to her mother and ate the rest herself. Not even one did she offer to Marushka. But on the third day she had tired of strawberries and fancied having some fresh, red apples.

"Run, Marushka," she demanded, "and fetch me fresh, red apples from the mountain."

"Apples in winter!" exclaimed Marushka. "Why, the trees have neither leaves nor fruit on them now."

"You idle girl! Go this minute, and don't come back unless you bring the apples."

As before, the widow added her commands and threats. The two seized Marushka roughly and turned her out of the house.

Poor Marushka went weeping through deep snow up the mountain till she came again to the fire around which sat the twelve months.

"Good men, may I warm myself at your fire?"

The great January raised his head and asked, "Why come you here? What do you seek?"

"I come to look for red apples," replied Marushka.

"But this is winter and not the season for apples," answered January.

"I know. But my stepmother and her daughter have ordered me to fetch them red apples from the mountain, and I dare not return without them. Pray, good sirs, tell me where to find them."

The great January arose and went to one of the elderly months, to whom he handed his wand. "Brother September, do you take the highest place."

September moved to the highest seat, which January had occupied. He waved the wand over the fire and a flare of red flames made the snow disappear. The trees leafed out, then

brightened with autumn colors. A frosty wind began to scatter the leaves through the forest.

Marushka looked about and spied an apple tree on which hung ripe, red fruit. She ran and shook the tree. One apple fell and then another. "That is enough," said September. "Now hurry home."

Marushka thanked the months and went down the mountain joyfully.

At home Holena and her mother marveled at the fruit. "Where did you gather these apples?" Holena asked.

"On the mountaintop," answered Marushka.

"Why did you not bring more?" said Holena fretfully. "You must have eaten them on your way back, you wicked girl."

"No, I have not even tasted them," declared Marushka. "I shook the tree twice. One apple fell each time. I was not allowed to shake it again, but was told to return home."

Holena would not believe her, and spoke so harshly that Marushka wept bitterly and took refuge in the kitchen.

Holena and her mother ate the apples. Never before had they tasted such delicious fruit. When they had finished the two apples, they both longed for more.

"Mother," said Holena, "give me my cloak and I will go fetch more apples. I will not send Marushka because the good-for-nothing wretch would eat them on her way. I will find the tree, and no matter who cries 'Stop!' I shall not leave until I have shaken all the apples from the tree."

Holena's mother brought a warm cloak and hood and helped her daughter put them on. Then Holena took the road to the mountain while her mother stood at the window and watched her disappear in the distance.

Snow covered everything and not a footprint was to be seen anywhere, but Holena pushed on until she reached the mountaintop. There were the flaming fire and the twelve months seated about it. At first Holena was frightened and she hesitated to go nearer. But then she went close and warmed her hands, without asking permission. The great January inquired severely, "What has brought you here? What do you seek?"

"I need not tell you," replied Holena. "What business is it of yours?"

January frowned and waved his wand over his head. Instantly the sky filled with clouds, snow began to fall, and the fire and the twelve months disappeared. Holena found herself alone in a wild storm. Although she tried to make her way home, she only wandered vainly hither and thither through the white forest.

Meanwhile, Holena's mother looked from the cottage window for her return. The hours passed slowly and she became alarmed. "Can it be that the apples have charmed her away from home?" she wondered. Finally, she put on her own hood and cloak and set out to search for her daughter. But the snow continued to blow in great drifts, covering everything. The icy north wind whistled through the mountain forests. No voice answered her cry. Neither mother nor daughter ever returned home.

Marushka lived on in the little cottage, and it and the field and cow became hers. In time an honest young farmer came to share them with her, and they were contented and happy as long as they lived.

Denmark

Ee-aw! Ee-aw!

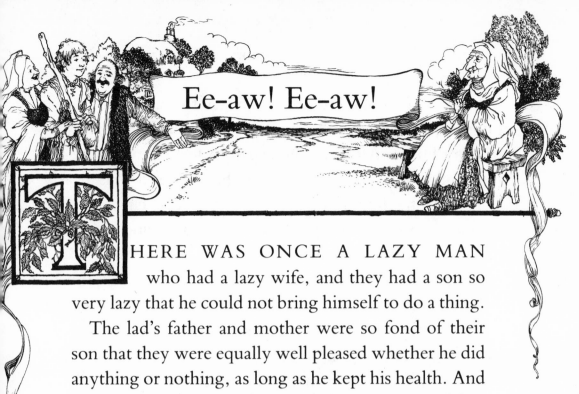

THERE WAS ONCE A LAZY MAN who had a lazy wife, and they had a son so very lazy that he could not bring himself to do a thing.

The lad's father and mother were so fond of their son that they were equally well pleased whether he did anything or nothing, as long as he kept his health. And he *did* keep his health. He grew tall and strong and fair; he was always pleasant and good-tempered, though he never cared to do a stroke of work.

When he was grown up, his parents began to discuss what should be done with their son. Something must be done, for he must be fed, and food was scarce at home. But it would be a sin to wish him to do any work; for *that* he had never had any liking, and to work well one must have some pleasure in working. So it was decided that he should go out and beg – that would be a way of life best suited to their dear boy.

Off he set, stick in hand and a beggar's pouch on his back. He walked slowly for there was no need to hurry. "Hurry brings worry," said he.

When he had gone a little way he began to feel hungry, so he sat down on the grass and ate what food he had brought with him from home. After that he began to feel sleepy, so he lay down under a tree to sleep. When he awoke it was nearly evening, but he thought he could go just a little farther before begging a night's lodging. As he was meandering along the road he met an old woman.

"Good evening," said she. "And where may you be going?"

"I am going begging," said he. "That is how I am to get my living. Work doesn't seem to suit me. But now, first of all, I must look about for a night's lodging."

"Well," said the old woman, who liked his manner, "I can direct you to the very place. Go into the first house you come to on your left hand. There you will get leave to stay if you will only do what I tell you. Before you go in you must pick up a little stone that you will see lying outside the door and put it in your pocket. And when you go in you must answer 'Thanks' to everything that is said, whatever it may be. And when the others are asleep you must put the little stone on the hearth, under the ashes where the fire is still glimmering."

"Many thanks," replied the youth, and he strolled on till he came to the first house on the left-hand side. He picked up the little stone that lay outside the door and went in. Here he saw a woman, so he wished her good evening and begged her to give him a night's lodging.

"No," said the woman, "I can't do that."

"Many thanks," said he.

"But I say that it can't be done," insisted the woman. "We don't give a night's lodging to strange folk."

"Many thanks," said he again, and seated himself on a bench. The woman let him sit there. She did not want to drive him out. Soon after this her husband came home.

"Who is that sitting there?" he asked.

"I haven't the least idea," said his wife. "He is either deaf or stupid, for I told him he could not stop here, and he only said, 'Many thanks.'"

The man said no more, but took his seat at the table, and his wife fetched the saucepan containing his supper. Placing the dish before him, she told him to eat as much as he wanted and she would put aside the remainder. As she said this, she never so much as glanced at the stranger.

"Thanks, thanks," said the youth, drawing up to the table

and helping himself so liberally to the supper that he left less than half in the dish.

Both the man and his wife were astonished, but they said nothing. She told her husband he could go to sleep as soon as he liked.

"Thanks," said their guest, and he took off his clothes and popped into the bed.

Before the man and his wife had recovered from their surprise, they heard him gently snoring. Being kindhearted people, they did not turn him out, but made up a bed for themselves on the floor.

As soon as they were asleep, the youth, who had only pretended to sleep, crept softly to the hearth and hid the stone amid the ashes. Then he returned to bed and went to sleep.

Now the people of the house had a daughter, a stout, buxom lass, just grown up. Always she was the first to get up in the morning and light the fire. This morning again she took the poker, stirred up the ashes, and laid fresh wood for kindling, but she could not get a fire to burn. When she stooped down to blow and opened her mouth, "Ee-aw! Ee-aw! Ee-aw!" was all she could say, and she couldn't stop saying it. The fire wouldn't burn and she could only sit down and cry, with tears and sobs, "Ee-aw! Ee-aw! Ee-aw!"

At this her mother awoke and asked what was the matter.

"Ee-aw!" replied the girl. "It won't – Ee-aw! Ee-aw! Ee-aw!"

"Well, and if the fire won't burn, is that the way to behave?" The mother got up and went to the hearth. She in her turn knelt down, stirred the ashes about, and was about to blow, when "Ee-aw! Ee-aw!" she cried. And now she too could not leave off saying it and could not get the fire to burn.

Mother and daughter screamed in concert, till the husband, waking, asked if they had both gone mad.

"Ah! Ee-aw! Ee-aw!" they both cried at the very top of their voices.

The man got up and found that they could not get the fire to burn. *That* was what all the noise was about.

"Ah!" said he. "Womenfolk don't know any better. They make a great fuss about nothing." He took the poker, stirred up the ashes, and was about to blow, when "Ee-aw! Ee-aw! Ee-aw-aw-aw!" he cried, just like the other two. And now all three screamed together.

Soon it was agreed that the girl should run to the parish clerk and ask him to come and say a charm over the bewitched fire. The girl ran with all speed to the clerk's house, and with great difficulty managed to stammer, "Please, Father says 'Ee-aw!' and Mother says 'Ee-aw!' and will you please come directly, and say a charm over the fire – Ee-aw-aw!"

The clerk thought the girl's manner rather odd, but he went with her. As soon as he had seen and heard the other two, he suspected something. There must be sorcery somewhere and it must be driven out. He took the poker and was about to work with the ashes, when the same thing happened to him that had happened to the others. He could say nothing but "Ee-aw! Ee-aw!" and he could not stop saying it.

The girl was sent out again, to the priest this time, and she arrived at his house very much out of breath. She said that the Evil One – "Ee-aw!" – had got into their house – "Ee-aw!" – and would the priest please come and read a charm over the fire – "Ee-aw! Aw-aw-aw!"

The priest put on his gown and his spectacles and followed the girl home. There he found them all standing by the hearth. The fire would not burn, and they were all crying "Ee-aw! Ee-aw!" at the top of their voices.

The priest opened his mouth, but the first words he uttered were "Ee-aw! Ee-aw! Ee-aw-aw-aw!"

What was to be done now?

The father began stammering that to anyone who could drive the evil spirit out of his house he would give his only daughter and leave him all he possessed at his death.

Now all this time the guest had remained in bed calmly looking on and listening to all the uproar. For a while he wondered what it could be about. But finally the meaning became clear. When he heard what the man promised, he jumped out of bed, ran to the hearth, snatched the stone out of the ashes, and threw it away outside the door. Then he clasped the girl in his arms and kissed her.

So the fire blazed up. They were free from the spell and so delighted that they all kissed the boy. It was their turn to say "Thanks" now.

Then came the wedding. The priest married them for nothing, and the clerk sang for nothing. And as far as anyone knows they all lived long and happily.

The Wonderful Pot

A MAN AND HIS WIFE were once living in a very small cottage—the smallest and poorest hut in the whole village. They were so poor that they often lacked even their daily bread. They had been obliged to sell nearly everything they had, but had managed somehow to keep their only cow. At length they decided that the cow, too, must go, and the man led her away, intending to take her to market. As he walked along the road a stranger hailed him, asking if he intended to sell the animal, and how much he would take for it.

"I think," answered he, "that a hundred crowns would be a fair price."

"Money I cannot give you," said the stranger, "but I have something which is worth as much as a hundred crowns. Here is a pot which I am willing to exchange for your cow." And he showed the man an iron pot with three legs and a handle.

"A pot!" exclaimed the cow's owner. "What possible use would that be to me when I have nothing to put in it? My wife and children cannot eat an iron pot. No, money is what I need and what I must have."

While the two men looked at each other and at the cow and the pot, the three-legged thing suddenly began to speak. "Just take me," it said. The poor man thought that if the pot could speak, no doubt it could do more than that. So he closed the bargain, took the pot, and returned home with it.

When he reached his hut he went first to the stall where the cow had been tied, for he was afraid to appear before his wife at once. He tied the pot to the manger, went into the hut, and asked for something to eat. He was hungry from his long walk.

"Well," said his wife, "did you make a good bargain at the market? Did you get a good price for the cow?"

"Yes," he said, "the price was fair enough."

"That is well," she returned. "The money will help us a long time."

"No," he sighed, "I received no money for the cow."

"Dear me!" she cried. "What did you receive, then?" He told her to go and look in the cow's stall.

As soon as the woman learned that the three-legged pot was all that had been paid him for the cow, she scolded and abused her husband. "You are a great blockhead!" she cried. "I wish I myself had taken the cow to market! I never heard of such foolishness!" Thus she went on and on.

But, "Clean me and put me on the fire," suddenly shouted the pot.

The woman opened her eyes in wonder, and now it was her

turn to think that if the pot could talk, no doubt it could do more than this. She cleaned and washed it carefully and put it on the fire.

"I skip, I skip!" cried the pot.

"How far do you skip?" asked the woman.

"To the rich man's house, to the rich man's house!" it answered, running from the fireplace to the door, across the yard, and up the road, as fast as its three short legs would carry it.

The rich man, who had never shared anything with the poor, lived not very far away. His wife was baking bread when the pot came running in and jumped up on the table. "Ah," exclaimed the woman, "isn't this wonderful! I need you for a pudding that must be baked at once." Thereupon she began to heap good things into the pot – flour, sugar, butter, raisins, almonds, spices, and so on. And the pot received it all with a good will. At length the pudding was made, but when the rich man's wife reached for it, intending to put it on the stove, tap, tap, tap went the three short legs, and the pot stood on the threshold of the open door. "Dear me, where are you going with my pudding?" cried the woman. "To the poor man's home," replied the pot, running down the road at a great speed.

When the poor couple saw the pot skipping back to them, with the pudding in it, they rejoiced. The man lost no time in asking his wife whether the bargain did not seem to be an excellent one, after all.

"Yes," she agreed. She was pleased and contented.

Next morning the pot cried again, "I skip, I skip!"

"How far do you skip?" they asked.

"To the rich man's barn!" it shouted, running up the road. When it arrived at the barn it hopped through the doorway. "Look at that black pot!" cried the men, who were threshing wheat. "Let us see how much it will hold." They poured a bushel of wheat into it, but it did not seem to fill. Another bushel went in, but there was still more room. When every grain of wheat had been given to the pot, it seemed capable of holding still more. But as there was no more wheat to be found, the three short legs began to move, and when the men looked around, the pot had reached the gate.

"Stop, stop!" they called. "Where do you go with our wheat?"

"To the poor man's home," replied the pot, speeding down the road and leaving the men behind, dismayed and dumbfounded.

The poor people were delighted. The wheat they received was enough to feed them for several years.

On the third morning, the pot again skipped up the road. It was a beautiful day. The sun shone so brightly that the rich man had spread his money on a table near his open window to allow the sunshine to clear the mold from his gold. All at once the pot stood on the table before him. He was counting his coins, as wealthy men like to do, and although he could not imagine where this black pot had come from, he thought it would make a fine place to store his money. So he threw in one handful of coins after another, until the pot held them all. At that very moment the pot jumped from the table to the windowsill.

"Wait!" shouted the man. "Where do you go with all my money?"

"To the poor man's home," returned the pot, skipping

down the road with the money dancing within it. In the center of the poor man's hut it stopped, and when its owners saw the unexpected treasure, they cried out in rapture.

"Clean and wash me," said the pot, "and put me aside."

Next morning the pot announced again that it was ready to skip.

"How far do you skip?" asked the man and his wife.

"To the rich man's house!" So it ran up the road again, never stopping until it had reached the rich man's kitchen. The man happened to be there himself this time, and as soon as he saw the pot he cried, "There is that pot that carried away our pudding, our wheat, and all our money! I shall make it return what it stole!"

The man flung himself upon the pot, but found that he was unable to get off again.

"I skip, I skip!" shouted the pot.

"Skip to the North Pole, if you wish!" yelled the man, furiously trying to free himself. But the three short legs moved on, carrying him rapidly down the road. The poor man and his wife saw it pass their door, but it never thought of stopping. For all that I know, it went straight on, carrying its burden to the North Pole.

The poor couple were now rich. They thought often of the wonderful pot with the three short legs that skipped so cheerfully for their good. But it was gone, and they have never seen it since.

England

Jack and the Beanstalk

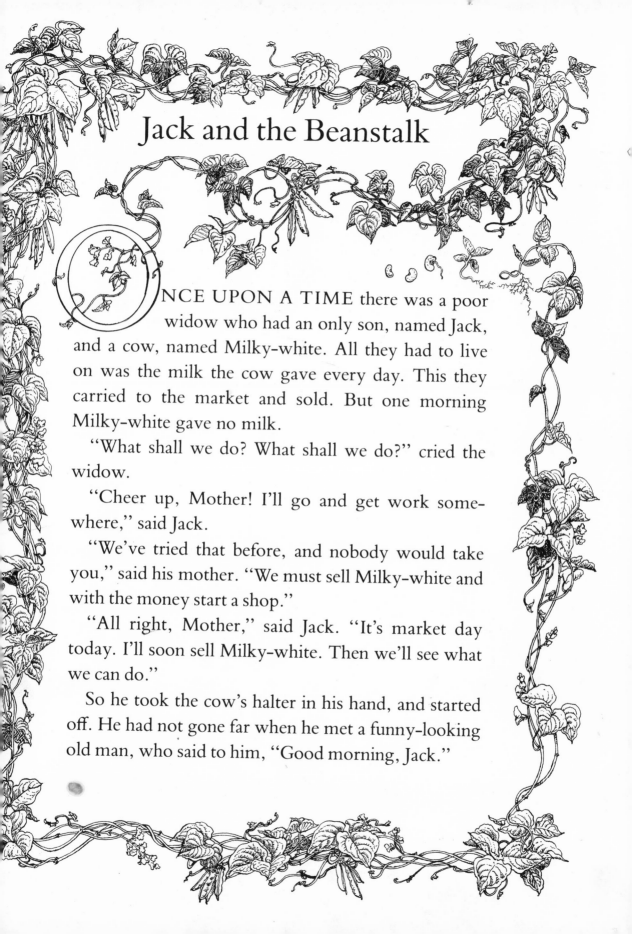

ONCE UPON A TIME there was a poor widow who had an only son, named Jack, and a cow, named Milky-white. All they had to live on was the milk the cow gave every day. This they carried to the market and sold. But one morning Milky-white gave no milk.

"What shall we do? What shall we do?" cried the widow.

"Cheer up, Mother! I'll go and get work somewhere," said Jack.

"We've tried that before, and nobody would take you," said his mother. "We must sell Milky-white and with the money start a shop."

"All right, Mother," said Jack. "It's market day today. I'll soon sell Milky-white. Then we'll see what we can do."

So he took the cow's halter in his hand, and started off. He had not gone far when he met a funny-looking old man, who said to him, "Good morning, Jack."

"Good morning to you," said Jack, wondering how the man knew his name.

"Well, Jack, and where are you off to?" said the man.

"I'm going to market to sell our cow."

"Oh, you look the proper sort of chap to sell cows," said the man. "I wonder if you know how many beans make five."

"Two in each hand and one in your mouth," said Jack, as sharp as a needle.

"Right you are," said the man, "and here they are, the very beans themselves." He pulled out of his pocket a number of strange-looking beans. "Since you are so sharp," said he, "I don't mind trading with you – your cow for these beans."

"Go along!" said Jack.

"Ah! You don't know what these beans are," said the man. "If you plant them at night, by morning the stalks will be right up to the sky."

"Really?" said Jack. "You don't say so."

"Yes, that is so, and if it doesn't turn out to be true, you can have your cow back."

"Right," said Jack. He handed over Milky-white's halter and pocketed the beans.

Back home went Jack. It was not dusk by the time he got to his door.

"Back already, Jack?" said his mother. "I see you haven't got Milky-white, so you've sold her. How much did you get for her?"

"You'll never guess, Mother," said Jack.

"No, you don't say so! Good boy! Five pounds? Ten? Fifteen? No, it can't be twenty!"

"I told you you couldn't guess. What do you say to these beans? They're magical – plant them at night and . . ."

"What!" said Jack's mother. "Have you been such a fool as to give away my Milky-white for a set of dry beans? Take that! Take that! Take that!" and she gave him three hard slaps. "As for your magic beans, here they go out of the window. Now off with you to bed. Not a drop shall you drink and not a bite shall you swallow this very night."

So Jack went upstairs to his little room in the attic. Sad and sorry he was, to be sure.

At last he dropped off to sleep.

When he woke up, his room looked very strange! The sun was shining, yet the room seemed dark and shadowy. Jack jumped up and ran to the window. What do you think he saw? Why, the beans his mother had thrown out of the window into the garden had sprung up into a big beanstalk. It went up and up and up till it reached the sky. The old man had spoken the truth after all.

The beanstalk grew close to Jack's window and ran up beyond like a great ladder. So Jack jumped onto the beanstalk, and began to climb. He climbed, and he climbed, and he climbed, and he climbed, and he climbed, and he climbed, and he climbed. At last, through the clouds, he reached the sky. When he got there he found a long, broad road going on as straight as an arrow. So he walked along, and he walked

along, and he walked along till he came to a great tall house. On the doorstep there was a great tall woman.

"Good morning, mum," said Jack, quite polite. "Could you be so kind as to give me some breakfast?" For he hadn't had anything to eat the night before, you know. He was as hungry as a hunter.

"It's breakfast you want, is it?" said the great tall woman. "It's breakfast you'll *be* if you don't move off from here. My man is a giant, and there's nothing he likes better than boys broiled on toast. You'd better be moving on or he'll soon be coming."

"Oh! Please, mum, do give me something to eat, mum. I've had nothing since yesterday morning, really and truly, mum," said Jack. "I may as well be broiled as die of hunger."

Well, the giant's wife was not half so bad after all. She took Jack into the kitchen, and gave him a chunk of bread and cheese and a jug of milk. But Jack hadn't half finished these

when – *thump! thump! thump!* – the whole house began to tremble with the noise of someone coming.

"Goodness gracious me! It's my old man," said the giant's wife. "What on earth shall I do? Come along quick and jump in here." She bundled Jack into the oven, just as the giant came in.

He was a big man, to be sure. At his belt he had three calves strung up by the heels. He threw them down on the table and said, "Here, wife, broil me two of these for breakfast. Ah! What's this I smell? . . .

"Fee-fi-fo-fum,
I smell the blood of an Englishman!
Be he alive, or be he dead,
I'll grind his bones to make my bread."

"Nonsense, dear," said his wife. "You're dreaming. Or perhaps you smell the scraps of that little boy you liked so much for yesterday's dinner. Here, go wash and tidy up. By the time you come back your breakfast will be ready for you."

Off the giant went. Jack was just going to jump out of the oven and run away, when the woman told him not to. "Wait till he's asleep," said she. "He always has a nap after breakfast."

The giant had his breakfast. After that he went to a big chest and took out of it two bags of gold. Down he sat and counted till at last his head began to nod. He began to snore till the whole house shook again.

Then Jack crept out on tiptoe from his oven. As he passed the giant, he took one of the bags of gold under his arm. Off he ran till he came to the beanstalk. He threw down the bag of gold, which of course fell into his mother's garden. He climbed down and climbed down till at last he got home. He told his mother what had happened and showed her the gold.

"Well, Mother," he said, "wasn't I right about the beans? They *are* really magical, you see."

They lived on the bag of gold for some time, but at last they came to the end of it. Jack made up his mind to try his luck once more at the top of the beanstalk. So one fine morning he rose early and got onto the beanstalk. He climbed, and he climbed, and he climbed, and he climbed, and he climbed, and he climbed. At last he came out on to the road again and up to the great tall house he had been to before. There, sure enough, was the great tall woman standing on the doorstep.

"Good morning, mum," said Jack, as bold as brass. "Could you be so good as to give me something to eat?"

"Go away, my boy," said the great tall woman, "or else my man will eat you up for breakfast. But aren't you the boy who came here once before? Do you know, that very day my man missed one of his bags of gold!"

"That's strange, mum," said Jack. "I dare say I could tell you something about that. But I'm so hungry I can't speak till I've had something to eat."

Well, the great tall woman was so curious that she took him in and gave him something to eat. But he had scarcely begun munching it, as slowly as he could, when – *thump! thump! thump!* – they heard the giant's footstep, and his wife again hid Jack in the oven.

Everything happened as it did before. In came the giant, roaring "Fee-fi-fo-fum," and had his breakfast of three broiled oxen. Then he ordered, "Wife, bring me the hen that lays the golden eggs."

So she brought it. Her husband said, "Lay," and the hen laid an egg all of gold. But then the giant began to nod his head and to snore till the house shook.

Now Jack crept out of the oven on tiptoe and caught hold of the golden hen. He was off before you could say "Jack Robinson." This time, the giant woke – because the hen gave a cackle. Just as Jack got out of the house, he heard the giant calling, "Wife, wife, what have you done with my golden hen?"

And the wife said, "Why, my dear?"

But that was all Jack heard, for he rushed off to the beanstalk and climbed down in a flash. When he got home he showed his mother the wonderful hen, and said, "Lay!" to it. It laid a golden egg every time he said, "Lay!"

Well, Jack was not content. It wasn't very long before he decided to try his luck again up there at the top of the beanstalk. One fine morning he rose early and stepped onto the beanstalk. He climbed, and he climbed, and he climbed, and he climbed, till he came to the very top. This time he knew better than to go straight to the giant's house. When he came near it, he waited behind a bush till he saw the giant's wife come out with a pail to get some water. Then he crept into the house and hid in a copper tub. He hadn't been there long when he heard *thump! thump! thump!* as before. In walked the giant and his wife.

"Fee-fi-fo-fum, I smell the blood of an Englishman!" cried out the giant. "I smell him, wife, I smell him."

"Do you, my dear?" said his wife. "Well then, if it's the little rogue that stole your gold and the hen that laid the golden eggs, he's sure to have got into the oven." And they both rushed to the oven.

But Jack wasn't there, luckily. The giant's wife said, "There you are again with your fee-fi-fo-fum! Why, of course, it's the boy you caught last night that I've just broiled for your breakfast. How forgetful I am! And how careless you are not to know the difference between alive and dead, after all these years."

So the giant sat down to his breakfast. Every now and then he would mutter, "Well I could have sworn . . ." And he'd get up and search the larder and the cupboards and everything. Only, luckily, he didn't think of the tub.

After breakfast, the giant called out, "Wife, wife, bring me my golden harp." So she brought it and put it on the table before him. "Sing!" he ordered, and the golden harp sang most beautifully. It went on singing till the giant fell asleep and began to snore like thunder.

Jack now got out of the tub very quietly and crept like a mouse over to the table. Up he crawled, caught hold of the golden harp, and dashed with it toward the door. But the harp called out quite loudly, "Master! Master!"

The giant woke up just in time to see Jack running off with his harp.

Jack ran as fast as he could. The giant came rushing after, and would soon have caught him, only Jack had a head start and knew where he was going. When he got to the beanstalk, the giant was not more than twenty yards away. Suddenly Jack disappeared. When the giant came to the end of the road, he saw Jack below climbing down for dear life.

Well, the giant didn't like to trust himself to such a ladder. He stood and waited, so Jack got another start.

But the harp cried out again, "Master! Master!"

The giant swung himself down onto the beanstalk, which shook with his weight. Down climbed Jack, and after him climbed the giant.

Jack climbed down, and climbed down, and climbed down till he was very nearly home. Then he called out, "Mother! Mother! Bring me an ax, bring me an ax!" His mother rushed out with the ax in her hand. When she came to the beanstalk,

she stood stock-still with fright. There was the giant with his legs just through the clouds.

Jack jumped down, took the ax, and chopped at the beanstalk, almost cutting it in two. The giant felt the beanstalk shake, so he stopped to see what the matter was. Then Jack chopped again. The beanstalk was cut in two. It began to topple over. Down crashed the giant, and that was the end of him!

Jack gave his mother the golden harp. With the magical harp and the golden eggs, Jack and his mother became very rich. Jack married a Princess, and they all lived happily ever after.

Tom Thumb

IN THE DAYS of the great King Arthur, there lived a mighty magician called Merlin. He was the most skillful wizard the world has ever seen.

This famous magician, who could take any form he pleased, was once traveling about as a beggar. Being very tired, he stopped at a poor cottage to rest, and asked for some food.

The countryman who lived there made him welcome. The man's wife, who was a very kind woman, brought him some milk in a wooden bowl and some coarse brown bread on a platter.

Merlin was much pleased. But he could not help seeing that the man and wife seemed unhappy, although everything was neat and snug in the cottage.

When Merlin asked them why they were so sad, the poor woman said, with tears in her eyes, "It is because we have no children. I should be the happiest person in the world if I had a son. Even though he were no bigger than my husband's thumb, I would be satisfied."

Merlin was so amused by the idea of a boy no bigger than a man's thumb that he decided to grant the poor woman's wish. In a short time, the farmer's wife had a son. And he was not a bit bigger than his father's thumb!

One night while the mother was admiring her child, the Queen of the Fairies came in at the window. The Fairy Queen kissed the boy and named him Tom Thumb. She then sent for some of her fairies, who dressed him as she ordered:

"A cap of oak-leaf for his crown;
A jacket woven of thistledown;
A shirt of web by spiders spun;
His trousers now of feathers done.
Stockings of apple-peel, to tie
With eyelash from his mother's eye;
Shoes made up of mouse's skin,
Tanned with the downy hair within."

Tom never grew any larger than his father's thumb, which was only of ordinary size. But, as he grew older, he became very clever and full of tricks. When he was old enough to play marbles with other boys he sometimes lost all his marbles. Then he would creep into the bags of his playmates to fill his pockets. Crawling out without being noticed, he would again join the game.

One day, as he was coming out of a bag of marbles, where he had been stealing as usual, the boy to whom the bag belonged saw him.

"Aha! my little Tommy," said the boy, "so at last I have

caught you stealing my marbles. You shall be punished for your trick."

He drew the string of the bag tight around Tom's neck and gave the bag such a shake that poor little Tom was in great pain. He cried out and begged to be let free. "I will never steal again!" he said.

A short time later his mother was making a batter pudding. Tom, being anxious to see how it was made, climbed up to the edge of the bowl. Then his foot slipped and he fell into the batter. His mother had not seen him. She stirred him into the pudding and put it in the pot to boil.

The batter filled Tom's mouth and prevented him from crying. But he kicked and struggled so much as the pot grew hot that his mother thought the pudding was bewitched. Taking it out of the pot, she threw it outside the door.

A poor tinker who was passing by picked up the pudding. Putting it into his bag, he walked off with it.

Tom had now got his mouth cleared of the batter, and he began to cry aloud. This frightened the tinker so much that he flung down the pudding and ran away. The pudding string broke. Tom crept out covered all over with batter and walked home. His mother was very sorry to see her darling in such a state. She put him into a teacup and washed off the batter. Then she kissed him and put him to bed.

Soon after this, Tom's mother went to milk her cow in the meadow and took Tom along with her. Lest the high wind should blow him away, she tied him to a thistle with a piece of fine thread. But the cow saw Tom's oak-leaf hat. She liked the looks of it and grabbed poor Tom and the thistle in one mouthful.

Tom was afraid of her great teeth and roared out as loud as he could, "Mother, Mother!"

"Where are you, Tommy?" asked his mother.

"Here, Mother, in the red cow's mouth."

His mother began to cry. But the cow, surprised at the odd noise Tom was making in her throat, opened her mouth and let Tom drop out. Luckily his mother caught him in her apron as he was falling down, or he would have been dreadfully hurt.

One day Tom's father made him a whip of a barley straw so that he could drive the cattle. Out in the field Tom slipped. He rolled over and over into a steep furrow of earth. A raven, flying over, picked him up and carried him out to sea. There it dropped him.

The moment Tom fell into the sea, a large fish swallowed him. Soon after, this very fish was caught, and was bought for the table of King Arthur. When the cook opened the fish in order to cook it, out jumped the tiny boy!

Tom was happy to be free again. The cook carried him to the King, who made Tom his special dwarf. Soon he grew to be a great favorite at court. By his tricks and fun, he amused the King and Queen, and also all the Knights of the Round Table.

The King quite often took Tom with him when he rode out on his horse. If it rained, Tom would creep into the King's pocket and sleep till the rain was over.

One day King Arthur asked Tom about his parents. The King wished to know if they were as small as Tom and whether they were well off. Tom told the King that his father and mother were as tall as anyone about the court, but rather poor. The King then carried Tom to the room where he kept all his money and told him to take as much as he could carry home to his parents. Tom, full of joy, at once got a purse.

But it would hold only one silver piece. Even this he could hardly lift.

At last he managed to place this load on his back, and he set forward on his journey home. After resting more than a hundred times by the way, in two days and two nights he reached his father's house.

Tom was tired almost to death. His mother carried him into the house.

During his visit Tom told his parents many stories about the court. One day, however, he decided he must return to the King.

Back at court, the King noticed how much Tom's clothes had suffered from being in the batter pudding and inside the fish, as well as from his journey. So the King ordered a new suit made for him. And he had Tom mounted on a mouse, like a knight, with a needle for a sword.

It was great fun to see Tom in his new suit, mounted on the mouse. When he rode out hunting with the King and his knights, everyone was ready to laugh.

The King was so pleased with Tom that he had a little chair made, also, so that Tom might sit upon his table. Then to live in he gave him a little palace of gold, with a door an inch wide. There was a coach, too, drawn by six small mice.

This way Tom was happy for a long time, and his parents were pleased with his success.

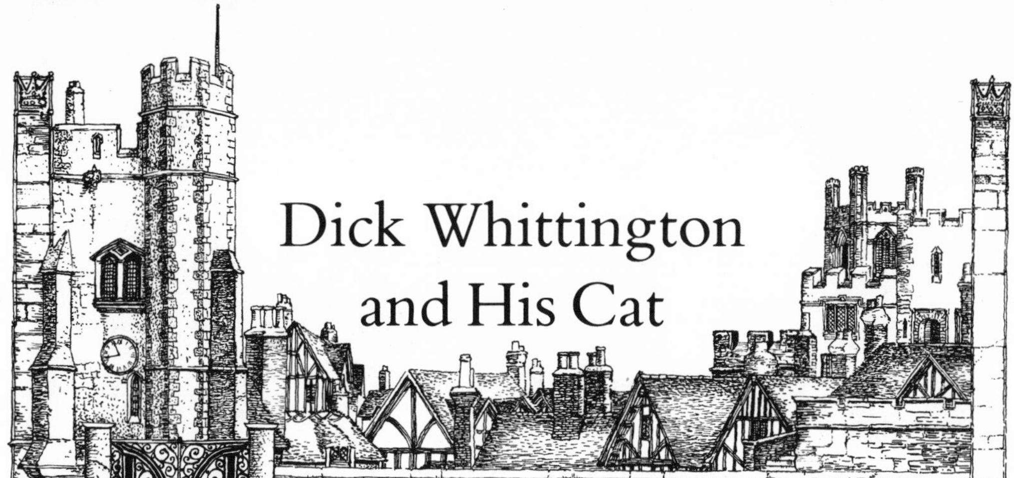

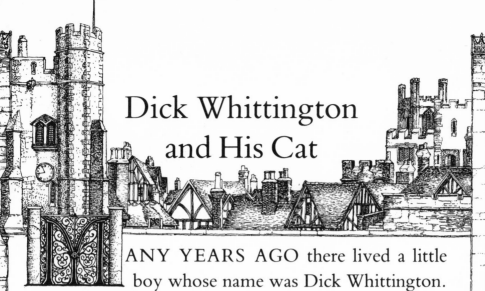

Dick Whittington and His Cat

MANY YEARS AGO there lived a little boy whose name was Dick Whittington. Dick's father and mother died when he was very young. As he was not old enough to work, he was very badly off. The people who lived in his village were so poor that they could spare him little more than the parings of potatoes and sometimes a hard crust of bread.

Dick had heard many strange things about the great city called London. The country people thought that folks there were all fine gentlemen and ladies. They believed that singing and music were heard all day long and all the streets were paved with gold.

Time passed till one day a wagoner was driving a large wagon through Dick's village on his way to London. Dick asked if he might walk with him by the side of the wagon. When the man learned that poor Dick had no father or mother, and saw by his ragged clothes that he could be no worse off than he was already, he told him he might go. So they set off together.

Dick got safely to London and ran off as fast as he could to look for the streets paved with gold. He ran until he was tired. At last, when it was dark and he had found every street covered with dirt instead of gold, he sat down in a corner and cried himself to sleep.

The next morning he got up and walked about, asking everybody he met to give him a coin to keep him from starving. Only two or three people gave him any money, and he was soon weak from hunger.

At length Dick laid himself down at the door of Mr. Fitzwarren, a rich merchant. Here he was found by the cook, who had a very nasty temper. She was busy getting dinner for her master and mistress, so she called out to poor Dick, "What business have you there, you lazy boy? If you do not take yourself away, we'll see how you'll like a sousing of dishwater. I have some hot enough to make you jump!"

Just then Mr. Fitzwarren himself came home to dinner. When he saw the dirty ragged boy lying at the door, he said to him, "Why do you lie here, my boy? You seem old enough to work. I am afraid you are lazy."

"No, indeed, sir," said Dick. "I would gladly work, but I don't know anybody, and I'm sick for lack of food."

"Poor boy, get up. Let me see what ails you."

Dick tried to rise, but had to lie down again, for he had not eaten in three days. The kind merchant then ordered him to be taken into the house and given a good dinner. He was to stay, to do what work he could for the cook.

Dick would have lived very happily with this good family if it had not been for the ill-natured cook. She would scold him, and beat him cruelly with a broom. At last her bad treatment was reported to Alice, Mr. Fitzwarren's daughter, who told the woman she would be turned away if she did not treat Dick more kindly.

The cook's behavior became a little better, but Dick suffered another hardship. His bed stood in a garret, where there were so many holes in the floor and walls that every night rats and mice ran over him. One day when he had earned a penny for cleaning a gentleman's shoes, he thought he would buy a cat with it.

He saw a girl with a cat, so he asked her, "Will you let me have that cat for a penny?"

The girl said, "Yes, that I will, though she is an excellent mouser."

Dick hid his cat in the garret, and always took care to take part of his dinner to her. In a short time, he had no more trouble with rats and mice, but slept soundly every night.

Soon after this, one of Mr. Fitzwarren's trading ships was ready to sail. It was the custom for all his servants to share in the profits of a voyage, so he called them into the parlor and asked them what they would send out to trade.

They all had something that they were willing to send, except poor Dick. For this reason he did not come into the parlor with the rest. But Miss Alice guessed what was the matter and ordered him to be called in. "I will lay down some money for him, from my own purse," she said.

But her father told her, "This will not do. It must be something of his own."

When poor Dick heard this, he said, "I have nothing but a cat that I once bought for a penny."

"Fetch your cat then, my lad," said Mr. Fitzwarren, "and let her go."

Dick went upstairs. With tears in his eyes, he brought down poor Puss. Giving her to the ship's captain, he thought, "Now again I'll be kept awake all night by the rats and mice." But Miss Alice, who felt pity for him, gave him money to buy another cat.

This kindness shown by Miss Alice made the cook jealous of poor Dick. She began to treat him more cruelly than ever, and always made fun of him for sending his cat to sea.

At last poor Dick could bear it no longer. He thought he would run away. So he packed up his few things and started off, very early. He walked as far as Holloway, and there sat down on a stone to think about which road he should take.

While he was considering this, the bells of Bow Church began to ring and seemed to say to him:

"Turn again, Whittington,
Thrice Lord Mayor of London."

"Lord Mayor of London!" said Dick to himself. "Why, to be sure, I'd put up with almost anything now – to be Lord Mayor of London, and ride in a fine coach, when I grow to be a man! Well, I will go back. I'll think nothing of the cuffing and scolding, if I'm to be Lord Mayor of London."

Dick did go back and was lucky enough to get into the house and set about his work before the cook came downstairs.

Now we must follow Puss to the coast of Africa. The ship, with the cat on board, was a long time at sea. At last it was driven by the winds to a part of the coast of Barbary. The Moors who lived here came in great numbers to see the sailors, and treated them politely. After they became better acquainted, the Moors were eager to buy the fine things that the ship carried.

When the captain saw this, he sent examples of the best things he had to the King of the country. The King was so pleased that he invited the captain to come to the palace. Here they sat on carpets woven with gold and silver, as was the custom. Rich dishes were brought in for dinner. However, a vast number of rats and mice rushed in too. These ate all the meat in an instant!

The captain learned that the King would give half his

treasure to be freed of the rats and mice. "They not only destroy his dinner," he was told, "but they attack him in his chamber, and even in bed. He has to be watched while he is sleeping."

The captain was delighted! He remembered poor Whittington and his cat, and told the King that he had an animal on board ship that would do away with all these pests at once. The King jumped so high for joy that his turban dropped off his head.

"Bring this animal at once," he said. "Rats and mice are dreadful! If she will do as you say, I will load your ship with gold and jewels in exchange for her!"

Cleverly, the captain set forth the merits of Puss. He told the King, "It is not very convenient to part with her, for, when she is gone, the rats and mice may destroy the goods in the ship. But, to oblige Your Majesty, I will fetch her."

"Run, run!" said the Queen. "I'm impatient to see the dear creature."

Away went the captain to the ship, while another dinner was made ready. He put Puss under his arm, and arrived at the palace just in time to see the table again covered with rats. When the cat saw them, she did not wait for orders, but jumped out of the captain's arms. In a few minutes almost all of the rats and mice were dead at her feet. The rest of them scampered away to their holes in fright.

The King was happy to get rid of the plague so easily. He was pleased, too, to learn that Puss's kittens would keep the

whole country free from rats. So he gave the captain ten times as much for the cat as for all the rest of the cargo.

The captain now could take leave of the court and set sail for England.

Early one morning Mr. Fitzwarren had just sat down to his countinghouse desk, when he heard somebody—*tap, tap*—at his door.

"Who's there?" said Mr. Fitzwarren.

"A friend," answered the other. "I come to bring you good news of your ship, the *Unicorn*."

The merchant opened his door. Whom should he see waiting but his captain and his agent with a cabinet of jewels! He looked at their report of the trading, and thanked heaven for giving him such a prosperous voyage.

He heard the story of the cat and saw the rich gifts that the King and Queen had sent to poor Dick. He called out to his servants:

"Go send him in, and tell him of his fame;
Pray call him Mr. Whittington by name."

Mr. Fitzwarren proved he was a good man. Some of his servants said that so great a treasure was too much for Dick. He answered them, "God forbid I should deprive him of the value of a single penny."

Dick was at that time scouring pots for the cook, and quite dirty. He wanted to excuse himself from coming into the countinghouse, but the merchant ordered him to enter.

Mr. Fitzwarren had a chair set for him. Dick began to think they were making fun of him and said, "Don't play tricks with me. Let me go back to my work, if you please."

"Indeed, Mr. Whittington," said the merchant, "we are all quite in earnest. I rejoice in the news that these gentlemen have brought you. The captain has sold your cat to the King of Barbary. In return for her you have more riches than I possess in the whole world. I wish you may long enjoy them!"

Poor Dick was so full of joy he hardly knew how to behave. He begged his master to take any part of the treasure that he pleased, since he owed it all to his kindness.

"No, no," answered Mr. Fitzwarren, "this is all yours. I know you will use it well."

Dick next asked his mistress, and then Miss Alice, to accept a part of his good fortune. But they would not. Dick was too generous to keep it all to himself, however. He gave presents to the captain, the agent, and the rest of Mr. Fitzwarren's servants – even to the ill-natured old cook.

After this, Mr. Fitzwarren advised Dick to send for a tailor and have himself dressed like a gentleman. He told him he was welcome to live in his house till he could provide himself with a better one.

When Whittington's face was washed, his hair curled, his hat cocked, and he was dressed in a fine suit of clothes, he was as handsome as any young gentleman who visited at Mr. Fitzwarren's. Miss Alice, who had once been so kind to him and thought of him with pity, now looked upon him as fit to be her sweetheart. Whittington thought always of how to please her, and gave her the prettiest gifts he could find.

Mr. Fitzwarren soon saw that they loved each other, and proposed to join them in marriage. To this they both readily agreed. Their wedding was attended by the Lord Mayor, the court of aldermen, the sheriffs, and a great number of the richest merchants in London.

Mr. Whittington and his lady lived on in great splendor and were very happy, with several children. He became Sheriff of London and thrice Lord Mayor, and from the King he received the honor of knighthood. Each time he became Lord Mayor, he recalled the sound of Bow Bells:

"Turn again, Whittington,
Thrice Lord Mayor of London."

France

Puss in Boots

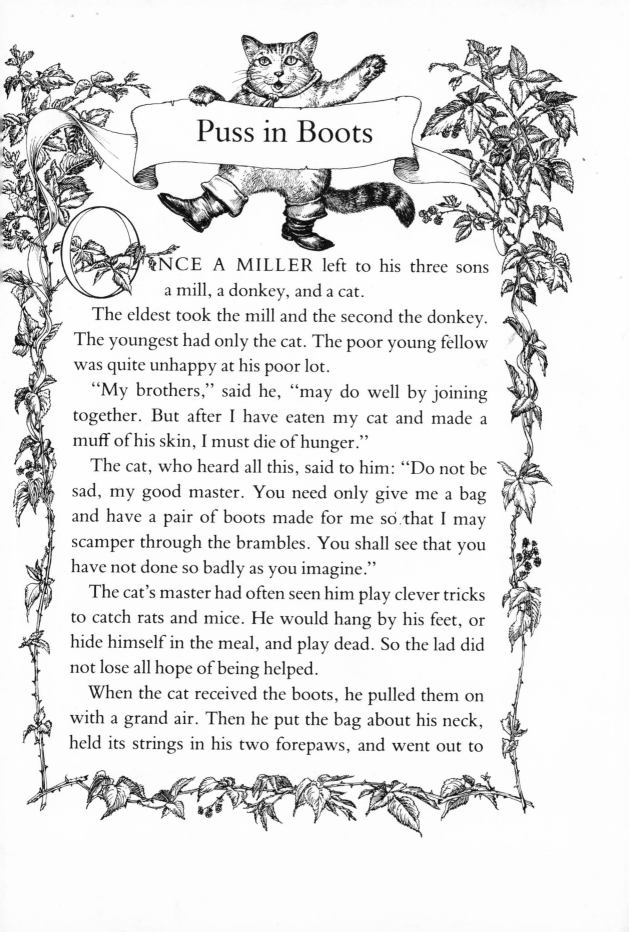

ONCE A MILLER left to his three sons a mill, a donkey, and a cat.

The eldest took the mill and the second the donkey. The youngest had only the cat. The poor young fellow was quite unhappy at his poor lot.

"My brothers," said he, "may do well by joining together. But after I have eaten my cat and made a muff of his skin, I must die of hunger."

The cat, who heard all this, said to him: "Do not be sad, my good master. You need only give me a bag and have a pair of boots made for me so that I may scamper through the brambles. You shall see that you have not done so badly as you imagine."

The cat's master had often seen him play clever tricks to catch rats and mice. He would hang by his feet, or hide himself in the meal, and play dead. So the lad did not lose all hope of being helped.

When the cat received the boots, he pulled them on with a grand air. Then he put the bag about his neck, held its strings in his two forepaws, and went out to hunt for rabbits. He put bran and lettuce into his bag and stretched out beside it as if he were dead. He waited for young rabbits, who had not yet learned the tricks of the world, to crawl into the bag and eat what he had put there.

Scarcely had he lain down when he gained what he wanted. A foolish young rabbit entered the bag. Puss, drawing close the strings, killed him without pity.

Proud of his catch, Puss carried it to the King's palace, and asked to speak with His Majesty.

He was shown into the King's rooms. Making a low bow, the cat said:

"I have brought you, sir, a rabbit, which my noble lord, the Marquis of Carabas"—that was the title Puss was pleased to give his master—"has commanded me to present to Your Majesty from him."

"Tell your master," said the King, "that I thank him, and that his present gives me a great deal of pleasure."

Another time the cat hid himself in a field of corn, holding his bag open. When a pair of partridges ran into it, he drew the strings and thus caught both of the birds. He gave them to the King as he had given him the rabbit. The King received the partridges happily, and ordered some money to be given to Puss.

The cat continued for two or three months to carry game to His Majesty. One day, when Puss knew that the King was to drive along the river with his daughter—who was the most beautiful Princess in the world – he said to his master, "If you will now follow my advice, your fortune is made. You have nothing to do but wash yourself in the river – I shall show you where – and leave the rest to me."

The Marquis of Carabas did what the cat advised, without knowing why. While he was bathing, the King passed by. The cat began to cry out as loudly as he could:

"Help! Help! My Lord Marquis of Carabas is drowning!"

At this, the King put his head out of the coach window. He saw that it was the cat who had so often brought him such good game. He told his guards to run at once to the aid of the Marquis of Carabas.

While they were dragging the young man out of the river, the cat came up to the King's coach. He told the King that as his master was washing in the river, some robbers had run off with his clothes. The Marquis had cried, "Thieves! Thieves!" several times but no one had heard him. (Actually, the clever cat himself had hidden the clothes under a great stone.)

The King commanded his men to run and fetch one of his best suits for the Marquis of Carabas.

The fine clothes suited the Marquis, for he was well built and very handsome. The King's daughter took a secret liking for the Marquis. When he cast two or three respectful and tender glances upon her, she fell deeply in love with him.

The King invited the Marquis of Carabas to come into the coach and take the air with them. The cat, overjoyed to see his plan beginning to succeed, marched on ahead. Meeting some farm workers who were mowing a meadow, he said to them, "Good people, you who are mowing, if you do not tell the King that the meadow you are mowing belongs to My Lord Marquis of Carabas, you shall be chopped as fine as mincemeat."

The King did not fail to ask the mowers to whom the meadow belonged.

"To My Lord Marquis of Carabas," they answered. The cat's threat had made them terribly afraid.

"You have a fine place," said the King to the Marquis of Carabas.

"Yes," replied the Marquis, "this is a meadow that always gives a good harvest."

The cat, still running on ahead, now met some reapers. He said to them, "Good people, you who are reaping, if you do not tell the King that all this corn belongs to the Marquis of Carabas, you shall be chopped as fine as mincemeat."

The King, who passed by a moment after, wished to know to whom all that corn belonged.

"To My Lord Marquis of Carabas," replied the reapers.

The King was still more impressed.

The cat, going on ahead, said the same words to all he met. The King grew astonished at the vast lands held by the Marquis of Carabas.

Puss came at last to a stately castle. The master of this was an ogre, the richest ever known. He owned all the lands that the King had been riding through.

The cat had taken care to find out who this ogre was and what

he could do. He asked to speak with him, saying smoothly that he could not pass so near his castle without paying his respects.

The ogre received him as politely as an ogre could, and made him sit down.

"I have been told," said the cat, "that you have the gift of being able to change yourself into any sort of creature. You can, for example, turn yourself into a lion or an elephant."

"That is true," answered the ogre roughly. "To prove it, I shall now become a lion."

Puss was so terrified at the sight of a lion so near him that he at once leaped out on the roof. And not without trouble and danger, because of his boots. These were of no use for walking upon the smooth tiles.

A little while later, when Puss saw that the ogre was no longer a lion, he came down and admitted he had been very much afraid.

"I have been told, also," said the cat, "but I cannot believe it, that you have the power to take on the shape of the smallest animal. I have heard, for example, that you can change yourself into a rat or even a mouse. I must say, I think this impossible."

"*Impossible!*" cried the ogre. "You shall see."

The ogre then changed himself into a mouse and began to run about the floor. Puss instantly fell on the mouse and ate him up.

Meanwhile, the King, as he passed the ogre's fine castle, desired to go into it. Puss heard the noise of His Majesty's coach running over the drawbridge.

He ran out and said to the King, "Your Majesty is welcome to this castle of My Lord Marquis of Carabas."

"What, My Lord Marquis!" cried the King. "And does this castle, also, belong to you? There can be nothing finer than this court and all that surrounds it. Let us go in, if you please."

The Marquis gave his hand to the Princess and followed the King, who went first. They passed into a great hall, where they found a magnificent feast. This the ogre had prepared for his friends. They were that very day to visit him, but now dared not enter, knowing the King was there.

His Majesty was as charmed with the Lord Marquis of Carabas as his daughter, who was so much in love with him.

The King said to the Marquis, "It is only for you to say, My Lord Marquis, whether you will be my son-in-law."

The Marquis, making several low bows, accepted the honor that His Majesty offered. That very day he married the Princess.

Puss became a great lord, and he never ran after mice anymore – except for fun.

The Sleeping Beauty in the Wood

ONCE UPON A TIME a King and a Queen were very unhappy because they had no children. As the years passed they grew sadder and sadder.

But at last, after many years, the Queen had a daughter. Everyone rejoiced, and a very fine christening was held for this Princess. She had, for her godmothers, all the fairies to be found in the whole kingdom – which were seven. They were invited in order that each should make her a gift, according to the custom for fairy godmothers. The King and Queen knew that in this way the Princess would grow up with the best qualities anyone could imagine.

After the christening, all the company returned to the King's palace, where a great feast was ready for the fairies. On the table before each of them was a magnificent setting of heavy gold – a spoon, a knife, and a fork, all made of pure gold with a pattern of diamonds and rubies.

As they were sitting down at the table, there came into the hall a very old fairy, who had not been invited. No one had seen her for more than fifty years, so she was believed to be either dead or under a spell.

The King ordered a place set for the old fairy, too, but he could not give her a spoon, knife, and fork of gold, because pieces had been made for only seven fairies. The old fairy fancied she had been insulted, and growled threats between her teeth.

One of the young fairies, who sat by her, heard how the old fairy grumbled. She feared the old fairy might give the little Princess a bad gift – so, when they rose from the table, she hid behind the hangings. The young fairy wanted to be last to speak, in order to undo, as much as she could, any evil that the old fairy intended.

Now all the fairies began to make their gifts to the Princess. The youngest, for hers, said that the Princess should be the most beautiful person in the world. The next said that she should have the wit of an angel. The third, that she should have charm in everything she did. The fourth, that she should dance gracefully. The fifth, that she should sing like a nightingale. And the sixth, that she should play all kinds of music perfectly.

The old fairy's turn came next. With her head shaking – more with anger than from old age – she said that the Princess would prick her hand with a spindle and die of the wound. This terrible gift made the whole company shudder. They all began to cry.

At this instant, the young fairy came out of her hiding place and said, "Be assured, O King and Queen, that your daughter shall not die. It is true that I cannot undo all of what my elder has just done. The Princess shall indeed prick her hand with a spindle. But instead of dying, she shall fall into a deep sleep, which shall last a hundred years. After a hundred years, a King's son shall come and wake her."

The King, to avoid this bad luck, at once forbade, on pain of death, anyone to spin or even to have a spindle in the house.

Fifteen years later, when the King and Queen were away at one of their country houses, it happened one day that the young Princess was running up and down the palace. She climbed from room to room and came finally to the top of the tower. Here there sat spinning a good old woman who had never heard of the King's command against spindles.

"What are you doing there, goody?" asked the Princess.

"I am spinning, my pretty child," said the old woman, who did now know her.

"Oh!" said the Princess. "This is very pretty! How do you do it? Give it to me, so I may see if I can do it, too."

But no sooner had she taken the spindle than it stuck into her hand, and she fell down in a swoon.

The good old woman cried out for help. People came from all sides and threw water on the Princess's face. They loosened her clothes, struck her on the palms of her hands, and rubbed her temples. But nothing would bring her to herself.

Now the King, who had returned, heard the noise and climbed to the tower. He recalled what the fairies had said. Knowing that it must be, he had the Princess carried into the finest room in his palace and laid upon a bed all embroidered with gold and silver.

One would have taken the Princess for a little angel, she was so very beautiful. Her fainting had not taken away the color from her face. Her cheeks and her lips were red. Her eyes were shut, but she was breathing softly. This proved she was not dead. The King commanded the court to let her sleep quietly till her hour of awakening should come.

At this time the good fairy, who had saved the life of the Princess by putting her to sleep for a hundred years, was far away in another kingdom. She learned what had happened from a little dwarf who had boots in which he could go seven leagues in one stride. The fairy left at once for the palace of the Princess. In an hour she was seen arriving, in a fiery chariot drawn by dragons.

The King handed her out of the chariot. She looked about and approved everything he had done. But, as she was very wise, she thought that the Princess, when it was time for her to awaken, would be greatly alarmed at finding herself alone in the palace. So she touched with her wand everything in the palace – the governesses, maids of honor, gentlemen, officers, cooks, errand boys, guards, pages, and footmen. She also touched all the horses in the stables, with their grooms. She touched the great dogs in the stableyard and little Pouffe, the Princess's spaniel, which lay close to her on the bed.

As soon as she had touched them, they all fell asleep. They would not awaken before the Princess needed them. The very spits at the fire, as full as they could be of partridges and pheasants, fell asleep; and the fire, also.

All this was done in a moment, for fairies are not long at their work.

Soon there had grown up all around the park such a vast number of trees, great and small, brambles and thorn bushes, twining one within another, that neither man nor beast could pass through. Nothing could be seen but the very tops of the towers, and those only from a great distance.

At the end of a hundred years, the son of the King then ruling, who was of another family, was out hunting. He was curious about the towers he saw above a great thick wood.

The Prince asked many people about this. Each one answered differently. Some said it was a ruined old castle, haunted by ghosts. Others said that witches had their night meetings there. The most common opinion was that an ogre lived there, who imprisoned all the little children he could catch.

The Prince was at a loss, not knowing what to believe, when a very old man spoke to him: "Many years ago I heard from my father (who had heard my grandfather say it) that there was in this castle a Princess. She was the most beautiful ever seen. She had been put under a spell, and was to sleep there a hundred years – until a King's son should waken her."

The young Prince felt all afire at these words. He went off at once to see if they were true. Scarcely had he advanced toward the thick wood when all the great trees, brambles, and thorn bushes gave way to let him pass. He walked up a long avenue to the castle. To his surprise, none of his people could follow. The trees closed behind him again as soon as he had passed through, but he went boldly on his way. A young Prince in love is always brave.

He came into a great outer court. What he saw there might

have frozen the most fearless person with horror. There was a frightful silence. Nothing was to be seen but stretched-out bodies of men and animals, all seeming to be dead. He knew, however, by the red faces of the guards, that they were only asleep. Their goblets, in which some drops of wine remained, showed plainly that they had fallen asleep while drinking.

The Prince then crossed a court paved with marble, went up the stairs, and came into the guard chamber. Guards were standing in rows with their guns upon their shoulders, snoring loudly. He went on through several rooms full of gentlemen and ladies, all asleep, some standing, others sitting.

At last the Prince came into a chamber all glittering with gold. Here he saw upon a bed the finest sight he had ever beheld – a Princess, who appeared to be about fifteen years of age, and whose bright beauty had something of heaven in it.

He approached with trembling and admiration, and fell down before her upon his knees.

And now, as the enchantment was at an end, the Princess awoke. Looking on the Prince with tender eyes, she said, "Is it you, my Prince? I have waited a long time."

The Prince, charmed with these words, and even more with the manner in which they were spoken, knew not how to show his joy and thanks. He vowed he loved her better than he did himself.

The Prince and Princess talked for four hours together, and yet they said not half of what they had to say.

Meanwhile all the palace awoke. Everyone thought about his own business. And, as they were not all in love, they were dying of hunger. The chief maid of honor grew very impatient and told the Princess loudly that supper was served.

The Prince then helped the Princess to rise. She was dressed magnificently, and His Royal Highness took care not to tell her she was dressed like his great-grandmother. She looked not a bit the less beautiful for all that.

Into the great hall of mirrors they went to dine. Violins and oboes played old tunes. The music was excellent, though it was now over a hundred years since the instruments had been played.

After supper, without losing any time, the Prince and Princess were married in the chapel of the palace.

In two years, the Prince's father died. The Prince and Princess became the new King and Queen, and were given a royal welcome at the capital.

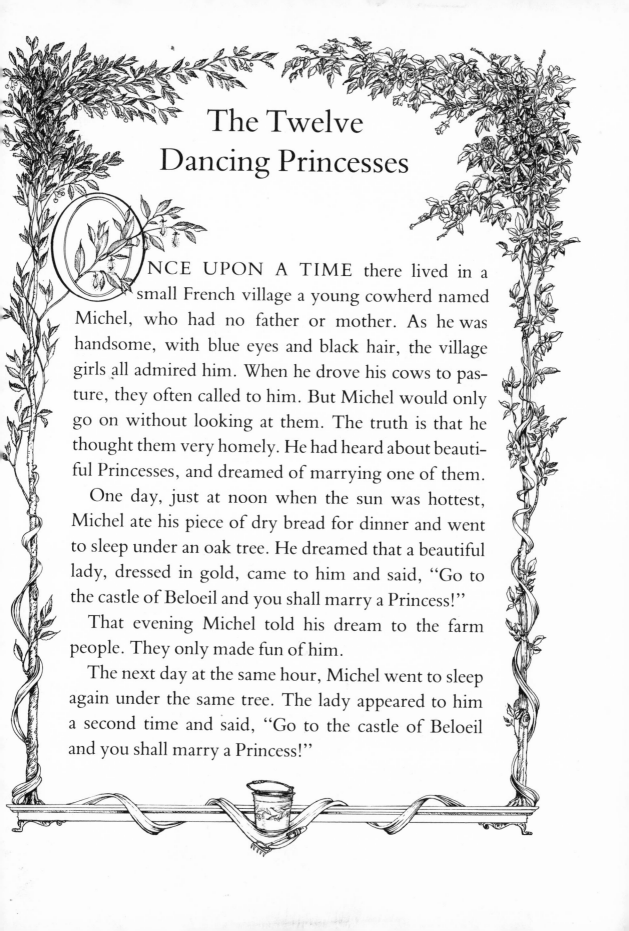

The Twelve Dancing Princesses

ONCE UPON A TIME there lived in a small French village a young cowherd named Michel, who had no father or mother. As he was handsome, with blue eyes and black hair, the village girls all admired him. When he drove his cows to pasture, they often called to him. But Michel would only go on without looking at them. The truth is that he thought them very homely. He had heard about beautiful Princesses, and dreamed of marrying one of them.

One day, just at noon when the sun was hottest, Michel ate his piece of dry bread for dinner and went to sleep under an oak tree. He dreamed that a beautiful lady, dressed in gold, came to him and said, "Go to the castle of Beloeil and you shall marry a Princess!"

That evening Michel told his dream to the farm people. They only made fun of him.

The next day at the same hour, Michel went to sleep again under the same tree. The lady appeared to him a second time and said, "Go to the castle of Beloeil and you shall marry a Princess!"

Again Michel told of his dream, and his friends laughed in his face. "Never mind," he thought; "if the lady should appear a third time, I will obey her."

The following day, about two o'clock in the afternoon, the little cowherd came down the road, singing as he drove his cows back early to the stable.

In a great rage, the farmer began to scold Michel, who only replied, "I am leaving."

Michel made his clothes into a bundle, said good-bye, and set forth bravely. Through the valley, toward the castle of Beloeil, he trudged on. He wondered what lay ahead for him.

There was, indeed, something important.

It was known that in the castle of Beloeil lived twelve beautiful Princesses. And they were as proud as they were beautiful, and so truly royal that they could feel a pea in their beds, even through ten mattresses.

It was known, too, that they lived like Princesses, and never rose until noon. Twelve beds they had, all in the same room. But what was most strange was that, though every night they were locked in by three bolts, every morning their satin shoes were worn out.

When asked what they did at night, the Princesses always answered that they slept. No one ever heard any noise, and no one could understand how the shoes wore themselves out!

At last the Duke of Beloeil had his trumpeter announce that whoever could discover how his daughters wore out their shoes should choose one of the Princesses for his wife.

On hearing this, a crowd of Princes came to try their luck. They watched all night behind the open door of the Princesses' room, but next morning the young men were gone, and no one could say what had become of them.

When Michel arrived at the castle, he went straight to the gardener and asked for work. The man had just dismissed his garden boy, so, although Michel did not look like a very strong boy, the gardener hired him. He thought the boy's good looks would please the Princesses.

Michel's first duty, when the Princesses arose, was to give each one a bouquet. He placed himself behind their door, with twelve bouquets in a basket. The Princesses took them without even looking at him – except Lina, the youngest, who admired him with her dark, velvety eyes.

Michel knew that all the Princes had disappeared while trying to learn the secret of the shoes. But Princess Lina's beautiful eyes gave him a great desire to try, himself.

Michel now had a new dream. The lady in gold came to him again, holding in one hand two young trees, a cherry laurel and a rose laurel. In her other hand she held a little golden rake, a little golden pail, and a silken towel.

She said to him, "Plant these little trees in two large pots, rake them with the rake, water them with the pail, and dry them with the towel. When they have grown as tall as a girl of fifteen, say to each of them, 'My beautiful laurel, with the golden rake I have raked you, with the golden pail I have watered you, with the silken towel I have dried you.' . . . Ask then for whatever you wish, and the laurels will give it to you."

Michel thanked the lady. When he awoke from his dream, he found the two laurels beside him. Carefully he obeyed the lady's orders.

The trees grew fast. When they were as tall as a girl of fifteen, Michel said to the cherry laurel, "My lovely cherry laurel, with the golden rake I have raked you, with the golden pail I have watered you, with the silken towel I have dried you. . . . Show me how to become invisible."

That evening, when the Princesses went to bed, Michel followed them, barefoot, and hid under one of the twelve beds.

The Princesses set to work opening cupboards and boxes. They put on the most beautiful dresses, and turned all around to admire themselves in their mirrors. From his hiding place, Michel could see nothing, but he could hear the Princesses skipping about and laughing.

At last the eldest said, "Be quick, girls; our dancing partners will be waiting."

When Michel dared peep out, he saw the twelve sisters splendidly dressed, with satin shoes on their feet, and in their hands the bouquets he had brought them.

"Are you ready?" asked the eldest.

"Yes," replied the other eleven, and took their places in line behind her.

The eldest Princess clapped her hands three times and a trap door opened. They all disappeared down a hidden staircase, and Michel hastened to follow. As he was walking close to Princess Lina, he carelessly stepped on her dress.

"There is someone behind me," cried the Princess, "holding on to my dress!"

"Stupid!" said her eldest sister. "You are always afraid of something. Some nail has caught your dress."

Down, down, down they went. At last they came through a passage to a door closed by only a latch. The eldest Princess opened it. They went out into a beautiful wood, where the leaves were spangled with drops of silver. Beyond that was another wood, where the leaves were sprinkled with gold. From there they went through a third, where the leaves were strewn with diamonds.

Michel saw next a large lake. On its shore awaited twelve little rowboats, decorated with flags. In each one sat a Prince, grasping the oars. Each Princess entered a boat, and Michel slipped in with Princess Lina.

The boats moved along rapidly. But Lina's, being heavier, lagged behind.

"We don't go so quickly as usual," said the Princess. "What can be the reason?"

"I don't know," answered the Prince. "I'm rowing as hard as I can."

Ahead lay a fine castle, splendidly lighted. From it sounded lively music. In a moment the boats landed. The Princes gave their arms to the Princesses, and they all entered the castle.

Michel followed them into the ballroom. The sight dazzled him – the mirrors, the lights, the flowers, and the rich hangings. Hiding in a corner, he admired the grace and beauty of the Princesses as they danced. He thought Lina, with her velvety eyes, the most beautiful and lovable. And how eagerly she danced! It was plain that she loved dancing better than anything else.

Poor Michel envied those handsome young men with whom Lina danced so gracefully. But he did not know how little reason he had to be jealous.

These young men were really the Princes who had tried to learn the Princesses' secret. The Princesses had given each of them a drink, to enchant them into forgetting everything but the love of dancing.

Everyone danced on till the shoes of the Princesses were full of holes. After a supper of the Princesses' favorite dishes, they went back to their boats.

Again they crossed the wood with the diamond-strewn leaves, the wood with the gold-sprinkled leaves, and the wood whose leaves were spangled with drops of silver. For proof of what he had seen, Michel broke off a small silver branch. Lina turned around at the noise it made.

"What was that noise?" she asked.

"It was nothing," replied her eldest sister. "It was only the screech of the owl at the castle."

Back at the castle, Michel slipped ahead and ran up the staircase, reaching the Princesses' room ahead of them. He opened the window and slid down a vine into the garden. Just as the sky was becoming light, he set to work.

That day, when Michel made up the bouquets, he hid the branch spangled with silver drops in the flowers for the little Princess. When Lina discovered it, she was much surprised. However, she said nothing about it.

In the evening, the twelve sisters went again to the ball. Michel followed and crossed the lake in Lina's boat. This time the Prince complained that the boat seemed heavy.

"It is the heat," replied the Princess. "I, too, have been feeling very warm."

During the ball, she looked everywhere for the garden boy, but in vain.

As they came back, Michel gathered a branch from the wood with the gold-sprinkled leaves. Now it was the eldest Princess who heard the noise it made in breaking.

"It's nothing," said Lina; "only the cry of the owl."

The next morning, Lina found the gold-sprinkled branch in her bouquet. This time she asked the garden boy, "Where does this come from?"

"Your Royal Highness knows well enough," answered Michel.

"So you have followed us?"

"Yes, Princess."

"How did you manage it? We never saw you."

"I hid," replied Michel.

The Princess was silent a moment. Then she said, "You know our secret – be sure to keep it!" She threw down a bag of gold pieces. "Here is something to keep you quiet." But Michel only walked away without picking it up.

For three nights, Lina neither saw nor heard anything unusual. On the fourth, however, she heard a noise in the wood with diamond-strewn leaves. The next noon there was a branch from it in her bouquet.

She took Michel aside and said to him, crossly, "You know what my father has promised to pay for our secret?"

"Yes, I know, Princess."

"Don't you mean to sell it to him?"

"No."

"Are you afraid?"

"No, Princess."

"What makes you keep quiet about it?"

Michel was silent.

Lina's sisters had seen her talking to the garden boy and made fun of her.

"What keeps you from marrying him?" asked the eldest. "You would become a gardener, too. It is a pretty profession. You could live in the cottage at the end of the park, and help your husband draw water from the well. When we get up in the morning, you could bring us our bouquets."

Then Princess Lina became very angry. When Michel gave her a bouquet, she accepted it coldly. Michel was most respectful and never raised his eyes to her. Yet nearly all day she felt him at her side without ever seeing him.

One afternoon Lina decided to tell everything to her eldest sister.

"What!" said that one. "This rogue knows our secret and you waited this long to tell me! I shall get rid of him at once."

"But how?"

"Why, by having him taken to the tower with the dungeons."

Lina and the eldest sister decided to discuss this with the other ten sisters. All agreed with the eldest that Michel should go to the tower.

Then Lina declared that if they touched a hair of the garden boy she would go and tell their father the secret of the holes in their shoes!

So instead it was arranged that Michel should go to the ball. At the end of supper he would take the drink, which would enchant him like the others.

Now Michel had been present, invisible, when the Princesses talked about this. He had made up his mind to take the drink. He would sacrifice himself thus for the happiness of the one he loved.

But, in order to look well at the ball, he now went to the laurels and said: "My lovely rose laurel, with the golden rake I have raked you, with the golden pail I have watered you, with the silken towel I have dried you. . . . Dress me like a Prince."

A beautiful pink flower appeared. Michel picked it. In a moment he found himself clothed in velvet as black as the eyes of the little Princess. The blossom of the rose laurel adorned his jacket.

Thus dressed, he went that evening to the Duke of Beloeil. The duke gave him leave to try to discover his daughters' secret. Michel looked so fine that no one recognized him as the garden boy.

The twelve Princesses went upstairs to bed. Michel followed. He hid behind the open door, waiting for the signal to leave. This time he did not cross in Lina's boat. He gave his arm to the eldest sister.

During the evening, Michel danced with each in turn. He moved so gracefully that everyone was delighted with him. At last, the time came for him to dance with the little Princess. She found him the best partner in the world, but he dared not speak a single word to her.

When the satin slippers were worn through, the fiddles stopped. The dancers all sat down at the banquet table. Michel was placed next to the eldest sister and opposite Lina.

The sisters gave Michel the most delicious food and drink, and the most flattering compliments.

At last, the eldest sister made a sign. One of the pages brought in a large golden cup.

Michel threw a last look at the little Princess. He accepted the cup and lifted it to his lips.

"Don't drink!" Lina suddenly cried. "I would *rather* be a gardener's wife!"

Michel at once flung the contents of the cup behind him. He sprang over the table and fell at Lina's feet.

The other Princes then fell likewise at the knees of the Princesses. Each chose a husband and raised him to her side. The charm was broken!

The twelve couples entered the boats, which had to cross back many times in order to carry over the other Princes. They all went through the three enchanted groves. When they had passed through the underground door, they heard a great noise, as if the fairy castle were tumbling down.

They went straight to the Duke of Beloeil, who had just awakened. Michel held forth the golden cup and revealed the secret of the holes in the shoes.

"Choose, then," said the duke, "whichever Princess you prefer."

"My choice is already made," replied Michel. He held out his hand to the youngest Princess.

But the Princess Lina did not become a gardener's wife. Instead, Michel became a Prince!

Germany

Rumpelstiltskin

THERE WAS ONCE a miller who was very poor, but he had a very beautiful daughter. It happened, one day, that this miller was talking with the King. To make himself seem important, he told the King that he had a daughter who could spin gold out of straw.

The King answered, "That would suit me well. If your daughter is as clever as you say, bring her to my castle tomorrow, so that I may see for myself what she can do."

When the girl was brought to him, he led her into a room that was full of straw. He gave her a wheel and spindle, and said, "Now set to work. If by early morning you have not spun this straw to gold, you shall die."

He locked the door and left her alone.

And so the poor miller's daughter sat. For the life of her, she could not think what to do. She had no idea how to spin gold from straw. Her plight was so hopeless that she began to weep.

Then all at once the door opened. In came a little man, who said, "Good evening, miller's daughter; why are you crying?"

"Oh," answered the girl, "I have to spin gold out of straw – and I don't know how to do it."

The little man asked, "What will you give me if I spin it for you?"

"My necklace," answered the girl.

The little man took the necklace. He sat down before the wheel, and – *whirr, whirr, whirr!* – three times around, and the bobbin was full of gold. Then he took up another, and – *whirr, whirr, whirr!* – three times around, and that one was full. So he went on till the morning, when all the straw was spun and all the bobbins were full of gold.

At sunrise, in came the King. When he saw the gold, he was astonished – and very pleased, for he was greedy. He had the miller's daughter taken into another room filled with straw, much bigger than the last. He told her that if she wanted to live she must spin all this in one night.

Again the girl did not know what to do, so she began to cry. The door opened, and the same little man appeared as before. He asked, "What will you give me if I spin all this straw into gold?"

"The ring from my finger," answered the girl.

So the little man took the ring, and began again to send the wheel whirring around.

By the next morning all the straw was spun into glittering gold. The King was happy beyond words. But, as he could

never have enough gold, he had the miller's daughter taken into a still larger room full of straw, and said, "This straw, too, you must spin in one night. If you do, you shall be my wife." He thought to himself, "Although she is but a miller's daughter, I am not likely to find anyone richer in the whole world."

As soon as the girl was alone, the little man came for the third time and asked, "What will you give me if I spin this straw for you?"

"I have nothing left to give," answered the girl.

"Then you must promise me the first child you have after you are Queen," said the little man.

"Well, who knows what may happen?" thought the girl. As

she could think of nothing else to do, she promised the little man what he demanded. In return, he began to spin, and spun until all the straw was gold.

In the morning when the King came and found everything done as he wished, he had the wedding held at once, and the miller's pretty daughter became Queen.

In a year's time, a beautiful child was born. The Queen had forgotten all about the little man – until one day he came into her room suddenly and said, "Now give me what you promised me."

The Queen was terrified. She offered the little man all the riches of the kingdom – if only he would leave the child.

But the little man said, "No, I would rather have a baby than all the treasures of the world."

The Queen began to weep, so that the little man felt sorry for her.

"I will give you three days," he said, "and if in that time you cannot tell my name, you must give me the child."

The Queen spent the whole night thinking over all the names she had ever heard. She sent a messenger through the land to ask far and wide for all the names that could be found.

When the little man came next day, she began with Caspar, Melchior, and Balthazar, and she repeated all she knew.

But after each the little man said, "No, that is not my name."

The second day the Queen sent to ask all the neighbors what their servants were called. She told the little man all the most

unusual names, saying, "Perhaps you are called Cow-ribs, or Sheep-shanks, or Spider-legs?"

But he answered only, "No, that is not my name."

On the third day, the messenger came back and said, "I have not been able to find one single new name. But as I passed through the woods, I came to a high hill. Near it was a little house, and before the house burned a fire. Around the fire danced a funny little man, who hopped on one leg and sang:

'Tomorrow at last the child comes in,
For nobody knows I'm Rumpelstiltskin.'"

You cannot think how pleased the Queen was to hear that name!

Soon the little man himself walked in and asked, "Now, Your Majesty, what is my name?"

At first she asked, "Are you called Jack?"

"No, that is not my name."

"Are you called Harry?"

"No," answered he.

And then she asked, "Perhaps your name is Rumpelstiltskin?"

"The devil told you that! The devil told you that!" shrieked the little man. In his anger he stamped with his right foot so hard that it went into the ground above his knee. Then he seized his left foot with both hands in such a fury that he split in two. And that was the end of him!

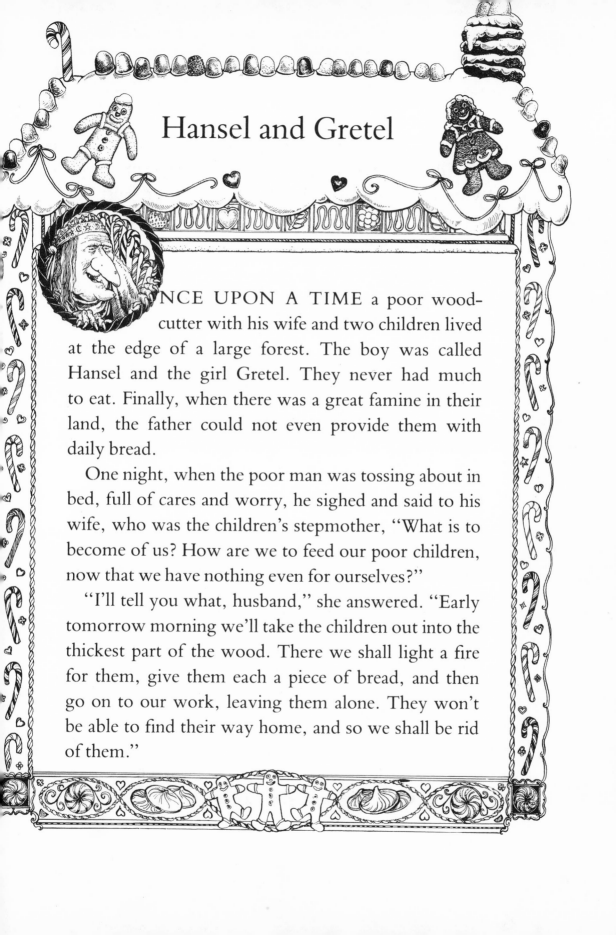

Hansel and Gretel

ONCE UPON A TIME a poor woodcutter with his wife and two children lived at the edge of a large forest. The boy was called Hansel and the girl Gretel. They never had much to eat. Finally, when there was a great famine in their land, the father could not even provide them with daily bread.

One night, when the poor man was tossing about in bed, full of cares and worry, he sighed and said to his wife, who was the children's stepmother, "What is to become of us? How are we to feed our poor children, now that we have nothing even for ourselves?"

"I'll tell you what, husband," she answered. "Early tomorrow morning we'll take the children out into the thickest part of the wood. There we shall light a fire for them, give them each a piece of bread, and then go on to our work, leaving them alone. They won't be able to find their way home, and so we shall be rid of them."

"No, wife!" said her husband. "That I won't do. How could I find it in my heart to leave my children alone in the wood? The wild beasts would come and tear them to pieces."

"What a fool you are!" she replied. "Then we must all four die of hunger." And she left him no peace till he consented.

"But I cannot help worrying about the poor children," added the husband.

The children were awake, for they had been too hungry to go to sleep. They heard what their stepmother said to their father. Gretel wept bitterly, "Now we're going to die, Hansel."

"No, no, Gretel," said Hansel, "don't cry. I'll find a way to help us."

When the old people had fallen asleep, Hansel got up, put on his little coat, opened the door, and stole out. The moon was shining brightly, and the white pebbles that lay in front of the house glittered like bits of silver. He bent down and filled his pockets with as many as would go in.

Then he went back and whispered to Gretel, "Don't fret, dear little sister. Go to sleep. God will help us." And he lay down in bed again.

At daybreak, even before the sun was up, their stepmother came and woke them. "Get up, you lazybones. We are all going to the forest to fetch wood."

She gave them each a bit of bread and said, "Here is something to eat, but keep it for your dinner, for you'll get no more."

Gretel put the bread in her apron, for Hansel had the stones in his pockets. Then they all set out together on the way to the forest. When they had walked a little, Hansel stopped and looked back at the house. He did it again and again.

His father noticed this and asked, "Hansel, what are you looking at, and why do you always lag behind? Take care and don't stumble."

"Oh, Father," said Hansel, "I am looking at my white kitten. It is sitting on the roof, waving good-bye to me."

His stepmother exclaimed, "Little fool! That isn't your kitten, it is the morning sun shining on the chimney."

But Hansel had not been looking at the roof. He had been dropping the little white pebbles on the path.

When they had reached the middle of the forest, their father said, "Now, children, pick up some wood and I'll light a fire to warm you."

Hansel and Gretel gathered twigs and soon made a huge pile. The wood was lighted, and when it blazed up their stepmother said, "Now lie down by the fire and rest yourselves, while we go and cut wood. When we have finished we'll come back to get you."

Hansel and Gretel sat down beside the fire, and at midday ate their little bits of bread. They heard the sound of an ax, so they thought their father was quite near. It was no ax, however, but a branch that was being blown about by the wind. They sat for such a long time that their eyes began to close, and they went fast asleep.

When they awoke it was dark.

Gretel began to cry, and said, "How will we ever get out of this forest?"

But Hansel comforted her. "Wait," he said, "till the moon rises. Then we'll find our way."

When the full moon had risen, Hansel took his little sister by the hand. They followed the pebbles, which shone like new pieces of money and showed them the path. All night long they walked, until at daybreak they found themselves back at their father's house.

When their stepmother answered their knock, she exclaimed, "You naughty children, why did you sleep so long in the wood? We thought you didn't mean to come back." The father was delighted, for his heart had been heavy at leaving them alone.

Soon, however, came another great famine. One night the hungry children heard their stepmother say, "We have eaten everything. The children must go. This time we shall lead them farther into the wood so they cannot find their way out again."

The father's heart was heavy. He thought to himself, "Surely it would be better to share our last crust with our children!" But his wife would not listen.

When their parents were asleep, Hansel again got up to go out to pick up pebbles. Now, however, he found the door locked, so he could not get out. He comforted his little sister by saying, "Don't cry, Gretel. Go to sleep. The good Lord is sure to help us."

In the early morning the woman made the children get up. She gave them each a piece of bread – even smaller than before.

On the way to the wood, Hansel crumbled his in his pocket and every few minutes stopped and dropped a crumb to the ground.

"Hansel, why are you stopping to look back?" asked his father.

"I'm looking back at my little dove, which is sitting on the roof waving good-bye to me," answered Hansel.

"Little fool, that isn't your dove," said the woman, "it's the morning sun shining on the chimney."

Hansel went on, dropping crumb after crumb until all the bread was gone.

The woman led the children still deeper into the forest, farther than they had ever been before.

After a big fire was lit, she said, "Just sit down here, children, and when you are tired you may sleep for a while. We are going farther on to cut wood. By evening we shall come back for you."

At midday Gretel shared her bread with Hansel, who had scattered his all along the way. Then they fell asleep. The evening passed, but no one came to get the children.

It was quite dark when they awoke. Hansel cheered his sister by saying, "Just wait, Gretel, until the moon rises. Then we shall see the bread crumbs I scattered along the path. They will show us the way home."

But these they could not see, even when the moon had risen. The thousands of birds that fly about the woods and fields had eaten every crumb.

"Never mind," said Hansel, "we shall find a way out."

The children wandered about the whole night, and the next day also, from morning till evening. But they could not find a path out of the wood. They became very hungry, for they had had nothing to eat but a few berries that they had found growing on the ground. At last they were so tired that they lay down under a tree and fell fast asleep.

On the third morning they were still wandering. Now they felt that if help did not come soon they would perish.

At midday they saw a beautiful little snow-white bird sitting on a branch. It was singing so sweetly that they stood still to listen to it.

When its song was ended, the bird flapped its wings and flew on in front of them. They followed it until they came to a little house, where it lighted on the roof. With delight, Hansel and Gretel noticed that the house was made of gingerbread. And it had a roof of cakes, and windows made of clear sugar.

"Now," said Hansel, "we'll have a real feast! I'll eat a piece of the roof, Gretel, and you can have a bit of the window. It will be good and sweet."

Hansel reached up and broke off a piece of the roof to see how it tasted. Gretel went to a window and began to nibble. At once a polite voice called out from within:

"Nibble, nibble, little mouse,
Who is nibbling at my house?"

The children answered:

"The wind, the wind,
The heaven-born wind."

And they went on eating.

Hansel, who very much liked the taste of the roof, tore down a big chunk for himself, while Gretel pushed a whole round pane out of the window and sat down to enjoy it.

Suddenly the door opened. An old, old woman, leaning on a crutch, hobbled out.

Hansel and Gretel were so frightened that they dropped what they had in their hands.

But the old woman only shook her head and said, "Oh, ho, you dear children! Who brought you here? Come in now and stay with me. No harm shall come to you."

She took them both by the hand and led them into the house. There she gave them a delicious dinner, of milk and sugared pancakes, with apples and nuts. After they had eaten, she showed them two pretty little white beds all ready for them. When Hansel and Gretel lay down, they felt as if they were in heaven.

Now, although the old woman seemed to be so friendly, she was really a wicked old witch who lay in wait for children to come by. She had built the house of gingerbread on purpose to lure them to her. Whenever she could get a child into her power, she cooked him and ate him and had a real feast day.

Witches have red eyes and cannot see far; but, like animals, they have a keen sense of smell and know when human beings pass by. When Hansel and Gretel fell into her hands, she had laughed wickedly and said to herself, "I have them now. They shall not escape."

The witch got up early in the morning, before the children were awake. When she saw them both sleeping so peacefully, with their round, rosy cheeks, she muttered to herself, "They will make a dainty tidbit." She seized Hansel with her bony hand and carried him into a chicken coop and barred the door. "You may scream as much as you like. It will do you no good."

She went back to Gretel, shook her awake, and cried, "Get up, you lazybones! Fetch some water and cook something good for your brother. He's locked in the chicken coop, to be fattened. When he's nice and fat, I shall eat him."

Gretel began to cry bitterly, but it was no use. She had to do what the wicked witch commanded.

The best food was now cooked for poor Hansel, but Gretel had only crab shells. Every morning, the old woman hobbled out to the yard and cried, "Hansel, let me feel your finger, so that I can tell if you are getting fat."

But Hansel always held out a bone. The old woman, whose eyes were dim, could not see. Always thinking it was Hansel's finger, she wondered why he fattened so slowly.

When four weeks had passed this way, the witch lost patience and would wait no longer. "Now, then, Gretel," she called. "Be quick and get some water. Hansel may be fat or thin. I'm going to cook him tomorrow."

Oh, how his poor little sister sobbed as she carried the water! And how the tears streamed down her cheeks! "Dear God, help us now!" she cried. "If only the wild animals in the wood had eaten us, at least we'd have died together."

"Stop crying," said the old witch. "It will do you no good."

Early in the morning, Gretel had to go out to fill the kettle with water and light a fire. "First we'll do some baking," said

the old witch. "I have heated the oven and kneaded the dough." She pushed Gretel toward the oven, from which flames were shooting. "Creep in and see if it is hot enough for the bread." She intended, when she had Gretel in the oven, to close the door and roast her, so that she might eat her, too.

But Gretel saw what the witch had in mind, and said, "How do I get in?"

"You silly goose," cried the witch, "the opening is big enough. See, I could get in myself." She crawled over and stuck her head into the oven. Gretel gave her a big shove and pushed her right in! Then Gretel closed the door and bolted it.

How the witch yelled! It was quite horrible to hear. But Gretel fled – and left the wicked witch to perish.

Gretel ran as fast as she could to the coop. She opened the door and cried, "Hansel, we are saved! The old witch is dead!"

Hansel sprang like a bird out of an opened cage. The children fell on each other, kissed one another, and danced about for joy. As they had nothing more to fear, they went into the witch's house and found, in every corner of the room, chests filled with pearls and precious stones.

"These are even better than pebbles," said Hansel, and crammed his pockets full.

"I must take some home with me, too," said Gretel, and filled her apron.

"But now we must leave this haunted wood," said Hansel.

On their way out, they came to a big lake. "We cannot get over this," said Hansel. "I see no stepping-stones, and no bridge of any kind."

"There is no ferryboat, either," answered Gretel. "But look, there is a white duck swimming. It will help us over, if we ask." So she called out:

"No boat, no bridge—alack, alack;
Please, little duck, take us on your back!"

The duck swam toward them. Hansel got on its back and told Gretel to sit beside him. "No," answered Gretel, "it would be too heavy a load for the little duck. It must take us over in turn."

The good bird did this. When the children had got over safely and had walked for a while, the wood seemed to become more and more familiar.

At last they saw their father's house in the distance. They began to run. When they reached the house, they rushed inside to throw their arms around their father's neck. The poor man wept for joy, for he had not had a single happy moment since he had left them in the wood. In the meantime his wife had died.

Gretel shook out her apron and scattered pearls and precious stones all over the floor. Hansel drew more handfuls of jewels out of his pockets. So, at last, all their troubles came to an end, and they lived together happily ever afterward.

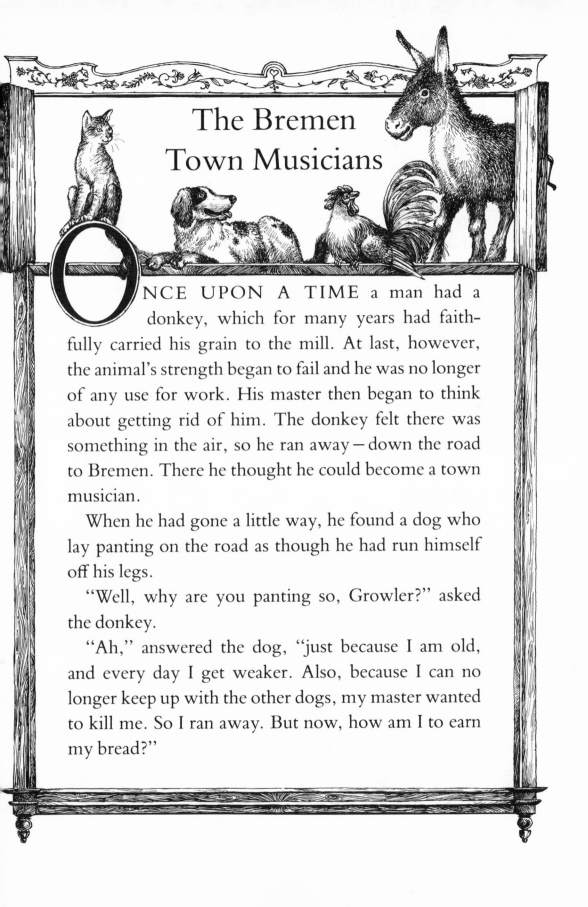

The Bremen Town Musicians

ONCE UPON A TIME a man had a donkey, which for many years had faithfully carried his grain to the mill. At last, however, the animal's strength began to fail and he was no longer of any use for work. His master then began to think about getting rid of him. The donkey felt there was something in the air, so he ran away—down the road to Bremen. There he thought he could become a town musician.

When he had gone a little way, he found a dog who lay panting on the road as though he had run himself off his legs.

"Well, why are you panting so, Growler?" asked the donkey.

"Ah," answered the dog, "just because I am old, and every day I get weaker. Also, because I can no longer keep up with the other dogs, my master wanted to kill me. So I ran away. But now, how am I to earn my bread?"

"Do you know what?" said the donkey. "I am going to Bremen. There I shall become a town musician. Come with me and take your part in the music. I shall play the lute, and you shall beat the kettledrum."

The dog agreed, and they went on.

A short time after, they came upon a cat, sitting in the road with a face as long as a wet week.

"Well, what has been bothering you, Whiskers?" asked the donkey.

"Who can be cheerful when his neck is in danger?" said the cat. "I am getting old, and my teeth are dull. I prefer to sit by the stove and purr instead of hunting around after mice. Just because of this, my mistress wanted to drown me. I ran away, but now I don't know what is to become of me."

"Come with us to Bremen," said the donkey. "You are a great hand at serenading. You can become a town musician."

The cat agreed, and joined them.

Next, the three passed by a yard where a cock was sitting on the gate, crowing with all its might.

"Your crowing goes through and through one," said the donkey. "What's the matter?"

"Why – because Sunday visitors are coming tomorrow, the mistress ordered the cook to make me into soup! Now I am crowing with all my might while I have the chance."

"Come along, Redcomb," said the donkey. "We're going to Bremen. You'll find a much better life there. You have a strong voice. When we make music together, it will be good."

The cock agreed, and they all four went off together.

They could not, however, reach the town in one day. By evening they arrived at a wood, where they decided to spend the night.

The donkey and the dog lay down under a big tree. The cat and the cock settled themselves in the branches. The cock flew right up to the top, which was the safest place for him.

Before going to sleep, the cock looked around once more on every side. Suddenly he saw a light burning in the distance. He called out, "There must be a house not far off, for I see a light."

"Very well," said the donkey, "let us set out and make our way to it, for we have little comfort here."

The dog thought, too, that some bones or meat would be just the thing for him, so they set off toward the light. They soon saw it shining more clearly and getting bigger and bigger, till they reached a robber's den all lighted up. The donkey, being the tallest, went up to the window and looked in.

"What do you see, Old Donkey?" asked the cock.

"What do I see?" answered the donkey. "Why, a table spread with delicious food and drink, and robbers seated at it enjoying themselves."

"That would just suit us," said the cock.

"Yes – if we were only there," answered the donkey.

The animals began to think about how they might drive the robbers out.

At last they hit upon a plan:

The donkey was to put his forefeet on the windowsill. The dog was to jump on his back. The cat would climb up on top of the hound, and last of all the cock was to fly up and perch on the cat's head.

So that was done, and at a given signal they all began to perform. The donkey brayed, the dog barked, the cat mewed, and the cock crowed. Then they dashed through the window, shattering the glass.

The robbers fled at this terrible noise. They thought that nothing less than a demon was coming, and ran into the wood in the greatest alarm.

The four animals now sat down at the table. They helped themselves and ate as though they had been starving for weeks. When they had finished, they put out the lights and looked for sleeping places, each choosing one that suited its own nature and taste.

The donkey lay down outside, the dog behind the door, the cat on the hearth near the warm ashes, and the cock flew up to the rafters. As they were tired from their long journey, they soon went to sleep.

When midnight was past, and the robbers saw from a distance that the light was no longer burning and that all seemed quiet, the chief said, "We ought not to have been scared so easily."

He ordered one of the robbers to go back to examine the house.

The robber found everything quiet, and went on into the kitchen to kindle a light. Taking the cat's glowing, fiery eyes for live coals, he held a match close to them so as to light it. But the cat would stand no nonsense. It flew at his face, spitting and scratching. The man was terribly frightened and ran away.

He tried to get out by the back door, but the dog, who

was lying there, jumped up and bit his leg. As the man ran on across the yard, the donkey gave him a good sound kick with his hind legs. The cock, who had been awakened by the noise and felt quite fresh and gay, cried out from his perch, "Cock-a-doodle-doo!"

Thereupon, the robber ran back as fast as he could to his chief, and said:

"There is a horrible witch in the house, who breathed on me and scratched me with her long fingers. Behind the door there stands a man with a knife, who stabbed me. In the yard lies a black monster, who hit me with a club. And upon the roof the judge is seated, and he called out 'Bring the rogue here!' So I ran away, as fast as I could."

From that time on, the robbers dared not go near that house, and the four Bremen musicians were so pleased with it that they never wished to leave it.

Greece

Constantes and the Dragon

ONCE UPON A TIME there was an old man who had three sons, all of whom were determined to go and learn a trade. So they set forth one day into the uplands in search of work.

When they discovered a field that had not been reaped, they said to each other, "Come, brothers, let us go in and cut the grain. Whoever owns it will pay us for our labor." They set to work, and while they were reaping, the mountains began to tremble, and they saw coming toward them a full-size dragon. Believing the dragon to be the owner of the field, they tried to work even harder.

The dragon came close and said, "Good morrow, my lads."

"Good morrow, master," they answered.

"What are you doing here?" asked the dragon.

"We found this field unharvested, and came in to cut the grain, for we knew that whoever owns it would pay us for our good labor."

They continued to work, and when they had cut half the grain, the dragon said to the youngest brother, who was called Constantes, "Do you see yonder mountain? There lives my wife. I want you to take this letter to her."

Constantes took the letter. But though he was the youngest, he was a cunning lad, and he decided that he would do well to read the letter before handing it to the dragon's wife. Thus on the way he opened it, and luckily, for he found these words: "The man I send you is to be killed at once. You must put him in the oven to cook, for I want him ready for my dinner when I come home tonight."

Constantes at once tore up this letter and wrote another: "My dear dragoness – When the young man arrives with this letter, I beg you to kill our largest turkey for him. And you must fill a basket with bread loaves, and send him back with this food for the laborers."

Now when the dragon saw Constantes returning, with a donkey heavily laden, he said to himself, "Ah, that fellow is a cleverer rogue than I!"

And to Constantes and his brothers he called out, "Come, friends, let us get through with this field quickly, and go to supper at my house so that I may pay you!"

Quickly they finished the reaping, whereupon the dragon led them away. Secretly Constantes said to his brothers, "You have four eyes among you, brothers; you must keep wide awake to note where we are going."

That night after dinner, when the dragon and his wife had

fallen asleep, Constantes got up and woke his brothers. Then he crept over to the dragoness and took her ring from her finger, gently so that she did not feel it. The brothers ran off and had nearly reached the town when the dragon woke up and looked for them – for he was hungry now and ready to eat them all. At that same moment the dragoness cried out that her ring was missing.

The dragon saw what had happened and sprang to his horse, to go in search of the brothers. He spied them just as they were entering the town, and called out, "Constantes, stop and let me pay you!"

But the brothers replied that they did not want the pay and went on into the town, paying no heed to the dragon's demand that they come back.

In the town they searched for work and in a short time they were all in business: the eldest as a draper, the second as a carpenter, and Constantes as a tailor.

After a time, the eldest brother became envious of Constantes because he had the ring. He decided on a plan to get rid of him.

He went to the King and said, "Please, Your Majesty, you have many riches in your palace, but if you owned the dragon's diamond coverlet, you would stand alone among the monarchs of the earth."

"But how am I to get it?" asked the King. "Who is clever enough to fetch it for me?"

The brother then answered, "Let Your Majesty issue a proclamation saying that whoever shall fetch the dragon's coverlet, you will make a great and mighty man. You must then summon my youngest brother, who is a tailor, and order him to get it for you. If he refuses, you will threaten to destroy him."

Accordingly the King issued a proclamation. But no one was brave enough to offer to go and fetch the coverlet. So the King had his vizier summon Constantes. He told Constantes that he must go to the dragon's home and steal his diamond coverlet – he would be destroyed if he refused.

What could poor Constantes do? He had no choice but to set out on this mission. As he walked along, he prayed, "May the blessing of my mother and my father stand me in good stead now!"

He journeyed on and soon met an old woman to whom he bade his usual courteous "Good morrow."

"The same to you, my son!" said she. "And whither away? You must know that whoever goes this way never lives to come back."

"The King has sent me to fetch him the dragon's diamond coverlet."

"Alas, my son, you will be lost!"

"But what can I do?"

"You must go back and tell those who sent you to give you three hollow reeds filled with insects. Then you must return to the dragon's house at night, when he is asleep. You will empty the reeds upon his coverlet. The dragon and his wife will not be able to endure the insects, so they will fling the coverlet over the window ledge and leave it hanging there. Then you must seize it and carry it off as fast as you can, for if the dragon catches you, he will eat you for sure."

The lad did exactly as the old woman told him, and he managed to run off with the coverlet.

When the dragon got up and discovered the coverlet missing, he called to his wife, "Where have you put the coverlet?"

"It's gone!" she cried.

"Ah, wife," said the dragon, "there is no one who can have taken it but Constantes." With that he again rushed to his stable, mounted his fastest horse, and in a short time caught up with Constantes.

"Give me that coverlet!" he demanded. "What trick have you been playing this time, you dog?"

But Constantes only replied, "What I have done thus far is nothing. Just wait for what I shall do to you next."

The dragon could not touch Constantes, for he was now entering the King's territory. Constantes was able to carry the coverlet to the King. The King's reward was an order for two suits of clothes.

After twenty days had passed, the jealous eldest brother went again to the King and said, "Please, Your Majesty, has Constantes brought you the dragon's diamond coverlet?"

The King answered, "Yes, indeed, and a very fine coverlet it is."

"Ah, Your Majesty, but if you had the horse and the bell that belong to the dragon, you would then have nothing more to desire."

The King could not resist this possibility, so he issued another proclamation. As before, no one dared to answer, so Constantes was summoned to court again.

This time the King commanded, "You must return to the dragon's home to fetch me his special horse and bell. If you do not succeed, I shall kill you."

Now what was poor Constantes to do?

He left the King, pondering how he could obtain the horse and the bell. He knew that the horse would neigh, the bell would ring, and the dragon would waken, to come down and eat him.

What could he do against the King's command? There was nothing for it but to set off as commanded. Fortunately, again he met the old woman.

"Good day," he said, but sadly.

"The same to you, my son, and whither away this time?"

"Don't ask," he said. "The King has ordered me to bring him the dragon's horse and bell, and if I don't he will kill me."

Again the old woman had a ready answer. "You must go back into town and ask for forty-one wooden plugs, for the bell has forty-one holes to be filled. Then you must hasten to the dragon's den. When you arrive, lose no time in plugging the holes in the bell – be sure you fill every one of them, for if you leave one unstopped, the bell will ring and the dragon will come out to eat you."

With care Constantes did all that the old woman told him to do, so that he was able to get the bell, and then the horse, and to run away with them.

When the dragon woke up, he discovered that his bell and his favorite horse were both missing. Again guessing what had happened, he mounted another horse and caught up with Constantes, close to the King's border.

"You villain," he cried. "Give back my horse and bell, and I will do you no harm."

But Constantes only replied, "What I have done so far is nothing. Just wait for what I shall do to you next."

The dragon ran, but Constantes ran, too, so that the dragon could not catch him. Constantes was able to reach the King and present him with the horse and the bell. The King, in return, ordered two more suits and Constantes went off about his business.

After another twenty days the eldest brother once more went to the King and asked whether Constantes had brought him the horse and the bell.

The King answered that Constantes had done so, and very fine indeed were the dragon's horse and bell.

"Ah, Your Majesty! Now you've got these. But if you had the dragon himself to exhibit, then you could want nothing more."

This idea delighted the King. At once he issued a third proclamation: "Whoever is able to bring me the dragon so that I may show him in public, to him will I give a large kingdom."

Constantes's master soon brought word to him that he was to go and fetch the dragon.

But Constantes answered, "How can I fetch the dragon? He would make an end of me."

But his master said, "You cannot refuse to go."

So Constantes arose and went on his way. And as he tramped along he met the same old woman again, and greeted her with a "Good morrow, mother."

"Good day, my son. Whither away this time?"

"I am ordered to fetch the dragon for the King, and if I don't bring him, the King will kill me. Do tell me what to do, for this time I am sure I shall lose my life."

The old woman again had a ready answer. "You must not be dismayed, my lad. Go back and tell the King he must provide you with these things: a tattered suit, a hatchet and saw, an awl, ten nails, and four ropes. And when you have received these things, and reached the dragon's property, you must put on the tattered garments and begin to hew down the tree that is outside the dragon's castle. When he hears the noise, he will come out and say, 'Good day to you! What are you laboring at, old man?' 'What do you think, my friend?' you must answer, 'I am working at a coffin for Constantes, who has died. I have been at work all this time and cannot cut the tree down.'"

Constantes repeated this while he got together the necessary tools, and then proceeded to the tree outside the dragon's castle. He began to hew away, and he worked until the dragon heard the noise of his hatchet and came out of his castle.

"What are you doing here, old man?"

"I am working at a coffin for Constantes, who has just died," he replied. "But I cannot cut the tree down."

At this the dragon looked pleased. "Ah, the dog! Well, I shall soon manage it."

When the old man and the dragon together had made the coffin, the old man said to the dragon, "Get in and let us see if it is big enough, for you are the same size as he."

The dragon got into the coffin and lay down, whereupon the old man picked up the coffin lid, to see whether it fitted, and when he had laid it on, quickly nailed it down and tied it tight. He lifted the coffin with the dragon in it onto the horse that he had hidden behind the wall, and away he rode with it.

The dragon of course began to yell out, "Old man, let me out! The coffin fits!"

But the old man answered, "Constantes has got you. He is taking you to the King so that he may exhibit you in public!"

He carried the coffin to the King and said, "Now I have brought you the dragon to exhibit for the enjoyment of Your Majesty and all the people. But I ask that you fetch my eldest brother to open the coffin."

The King did as Constantes asked, and all his people gathered to look at the dragon.

When the eldest brother opened the coffin, the dragon, finding no one near him except the man who opened the lid, swallowed him in one gulp. This indeed was an exhibition—for all the crowd looking on from the casements and balconies of the palace. And it satisfied the King.

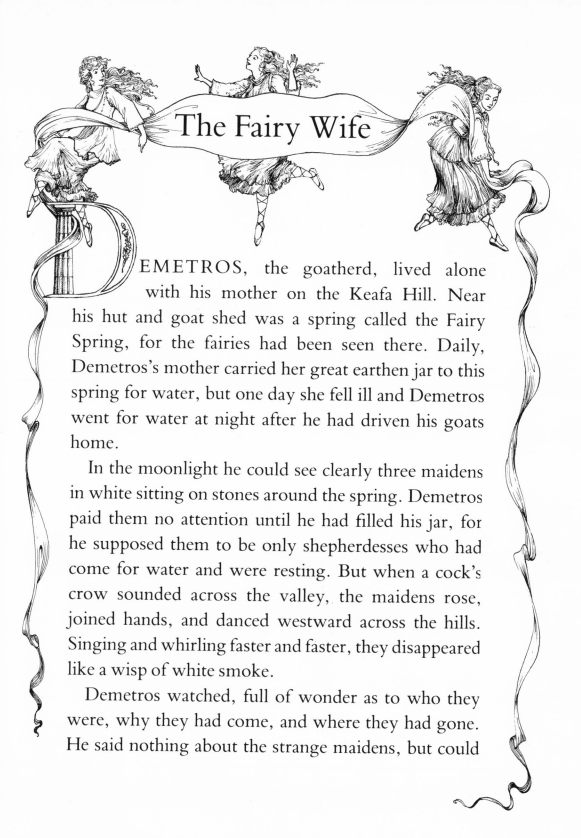

The Fairy Wife

DEMETROS, the goatherd, lived alone with his mother on the Keafa Hill. Near his hut and goat shed was a spring called the Fairy Spring, for the fairies had been seen there. Daily, Demetros's mother carried her great earthen jar to this spring for water, but one day she fell ill and Demetros went for water at night after he had driven his goats home.

In the moonlight he could see clearly three maidens in white sitting on stones around the spring. Demetros paid them no attention until he had filled his jar, for he supposed them to be only shepherdesses who had come for water and were resting. But when a cock's crow sounded across the valley, the maidens rose, joined hands, and danced westward across the hills. Singing and whirling faster and faster, they disappeared like a wisp of white smoke.

Demetros watched, full of wonder as to who they were, why they had come, and where they had gone. He said nothing about the strange maidens, but could think of nothing else all the next day. And at night he went again to the spring. In the moonlight he saw six maidens this time, and once again as the cock crowed they rose, danced singing over the hills, and vanished.

Demetros filled his water jar and walked home, thinking. He was so quiet his mother asked if anything was wrong. He hesitated, then told her what he had seen on the two evenings.

"Beware, my son! The maidens may be fairies. Evil may come!"

For the third time Demetros went to the spring, and this time found nine maidens sitting on the stones. Once again the cock crowed and they danced away.

"Surely there can be no harm in watching them. They are so strange, so beautiful!"

This time Demetros forgot to fill his water jar and walked home with his eyes on the far hills where the fairies had disappeared.

"You must have seen the maidens again!" his mother cried, when she saw the empty jar. "Tomorrow night brings the full moon when the fairies' power is greatest. Then you must not leave the goat shed."

Demetros intended to obey his mother, but all day as he watched his goats he thought of the maidens.

"I will not go tonight," he told himself. "I will never see them again. I do not want to see them. They might bring evil to my mother and me. I will not see them – but how beautiful they were!"

That night he put his goats into the shed as usual. Outside

the door he looked up at the full moon and remembered the last three nights. How lightly the maidens had danced! How brightly their golden hair had rippled over their shoulders!

It was now almost midnight, and before Demetros knew what he was doing, he found himself hurrying toward the spring. He tried to stop but he could not. He reached the spring and this time found ten maidens waiting for him. He had found the nine maidens of the night before lovely, but the tenth one they had brought with them now was many times fairer. She was more graceful, her hair was brighter, her face more beautiful than any maiden Demetros had ever imagined.

The ten maidens rose, joined hands in a circle about Demetros, and danced around and around, never touching the ground. And they sang a song that he could understand:

"Oh, to be light and oh, to be light
In the summer noonday sun;
On the sea sands bright and the hill snows white,
To run and to run and to run!

"Oh, to be gay and oh, to be gay
Where bright rivers glide and glance;
In gardens of May to skip and play,
To dance and to dance and to dance!

"Oh, to be free and oh, to be free
As the north wind riding high;
Oh, swift and free and a fairy to be,
To fly and to fly and to fly!"

Demetros longed to be as light and gay and free as they.

"Come with us," begged the ten maidens. "Come with us, Demetros."

"Come and live in our palace with us," said the tenth fairy with her loveliest smile. "We shall make you happy, Demetros."

Unable to resist, he went with them a long way over the hills. He laughed and sang and forgot everything but the fairy maidens, their flowers, their smiles, their golden hair. Once he thought of his mother, ill and in need of him, and of his goats that would cry for him in the morning. He knew he should not go farther with the fairies, but when he looked at the tenth, the most beautiful one, he felt that he could not leave her as long as he lived.

Now she came near him in the dance. Her long golden hair swept past him. He breathed the fragrance of her flowers. He reached out to catch her, but caught only her handkerchief. At that moment the dance stopped and the fairies screamed. With a rush, like wind through a forest, they disappeared – all but the tenth. She sank down and hid her face in her hands.

For a long time Demetros stood looking down at this fairy maiden who had become his prisoner. He fell to his knees beside her and tried to comfort her, but nothing could stop her tears.

"Do not speak. Do not touch me," she said. "You have robbed me of my freedom, my happiness!"

Demetros stood up, tucked the handkerchief into his wide leather belt, and walked slowly away, full of wonder again.

Looking back, he saw that she had risen and was following him, still weeping. He continued to walk, and she came, too, stopping when he stopped, moving forward as he did, until they had crossed the hills to his little hut.

Demetros's mother was startled to see this strange golden-haired maiden with her son. She welcomed her because she saw that Demetros loved her. She took the fairy handkerchief, wrapped it in silk, and locked it in her box away from the fairy wife.

Katena, as the beautiful fairy was called, spent her time now spinning, sewing, and embroidering. She made fine clothes for Demetros's mother, for herself, and for the little child that came to her and Demetros. Everyone in their village of Loutro knew that Katena was a fairy, because whatever she did was better work than anyone else could do in all their part of the country. The child, too, was very beautiful, with fine, golden hair. All the villagers and country people called her Neraidokoretso, which means fairy child.

But Katena was not happy, and nothing Demetros could do would make her smile. She never danced now or sang, but sat quietly at her work, scarcely speaking to anyone. Demetros grew sad, too, and to see him so unhappy made his mother grieve. This continued for seven years.

One St. Konstantinos Day, Demetros's mother went to a neighboring village to visit a cousin. She believed everything would be safe till her return.

But Katena said to Demetros, "Today is a holiday. I should like very much to go to Loutro to dance. I have not danced for a long time. Will you bring me one of my pretty dresses and my best handkerchief? We shall dance together as we danced under the full moon seven years ago."

Demetros could not speak for delight. His beautiful wife would dance and be happy again! He fumbled with the keys his mother had left in his care. He caught up the first dress his eyes fell upon. At length he found the beautiful handkerchief in his mother's box and with trembling hands folded it inside his belt. As soon as Katena was ready, she and Demetros with Neraidokoretso hastened down the hillside to Loutro.

In their bright costumes, joyous and graceful, the folk were already dancing on the grass plot in the center of the village. They formed a great circle, but instead of joining hands they faced each other in pairs, holding a handkerchief stretched between each two of them. Katena and Demetros stepped into the circle, holding between them the fairy handkerchief that his mother had guarded these seven years.

Katena's turn came to lead the dance. Demetros dropped his corner of the handkerchief and at once Katena sprang away, whirling madly about the circle. As Demetros watched her, amazed, she circled three times before the astonished villagers, then rose as though on wings and floated into the sky.

Demetros knew that his fairy wife had left him forever, and he wanted to die. His mother, returning from her cousin's, tried to console him. "My son," she said, "this is the evil that the fairy has brought upon us. Let us try to be content. Now nothing worse can come to us."

Demetros feared that his daughter would be unhappy without her mother, but every morning the child would hurry away to the fields and in the evening run home again, skipping and singing as she came. People said they often heard her talking or chanting to herself in words no one could understand.

Her grandmother was frightened at first because she could not induce the child to eat. One morning Demetros followed Neraidokoretso. He saw her go straight to the Fairy Spring and, looking up, hold her little arms toward the sky. He heard her calling and saw a white mist descend to her. A voice came out of the mist, and the child answered in words of a strange sound.

"It is Katena," he told his mother. "She must come every day to talk to Neraidokoretso and feed her fairy food. That is why she is in the fields all day and will eat nothing here. Katena is caring for her child."

As the years went by, Neraidokoretso grew more lovely, and more like her mother. When she went to the fields now she took her sewing or embroidery and worked while she talked with the spirit that no one else could see. Often Demetros followed her and watched. She was his daughter, but she never seemed to belong to him. She did not need him and was happy without him. It made him afraid, so that one day he said to his mother, "I believe something can happen to us worse than the trouble we have already suffered."

"How can that be, my son?" she asked.

"I am afraid that Neraidokoretso will not always be with us."

Demetros and his mother looked at each other without speaking. They both loved Neraidokoretso very much.

On the girl's fifteenth birthday Demetros followed her to the Fairy Spring, as he had done every day for so long a time. Again he saw the white mist come to her out of the clouds and heard the sweet voice. Today when she held up her arms, the mist enfolded her, lifted her up, and carried her away. After it had vanished, Demetros caught the echo of two fairy voices. He knew that Katena and Neraidokoretso had gone from him forever.

No longer did Demetros tend his goats. He wandered day after day through the fields and woods and over the hills, looking hopelessly for his wife and child. Sometimes a shepherd or goatherd, meeting him, would hear him chanting to himself:

"Come back, come back, my fairy wife.
Come back, my fairy child.
Seeking and searching I spend my life;
I wander lone and wild.
Come back!"

India

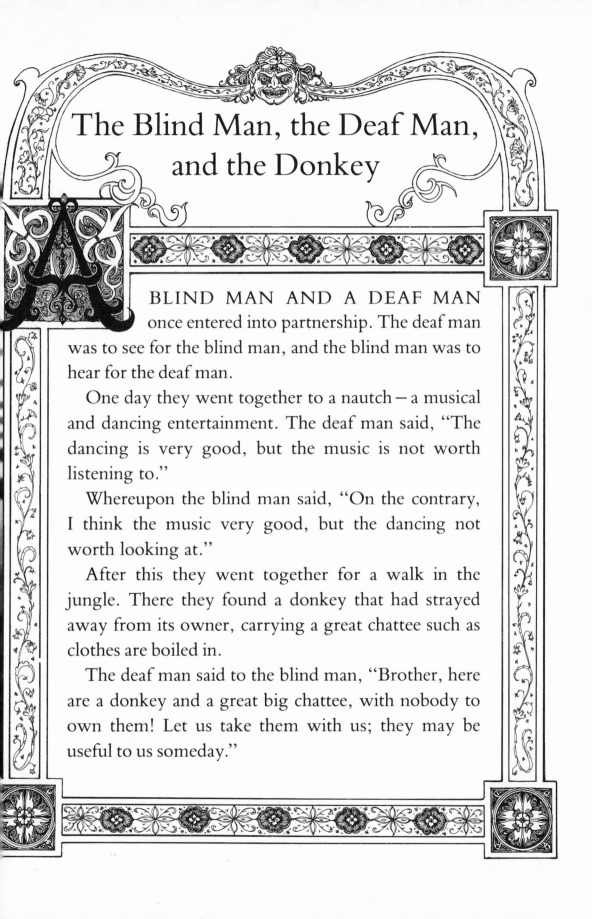

The Blind Man, the Deaf Man, and the Donkey

A BLIND MAN AND A DEAF MAN once entered into partnership. The deaf man was to see for the blind man, and the blind man was to hear for the deaf man.

One day they went together to a nautch – a musical and dancing entertainment. The deaf man said, "The dancing is very good, but the music is not worth listening to."

Whereupon the blind man said, "On the contrary, I think the music very good, but the dancing not worth looking at."

After this they went together for a walk in the jungle. There they found a donkey that had strayed away from its owner, carrying a great chattee such as clothes are boiled in.

The deaf man said to the blind man, "Brother, here are a donkey and a great big chattee, with nobody to own them! Let us take them with us; they may be useful to us someday."

"Very well," said the blind man, nodding his head, "we will take them with us."

So the blind man and the deaf man went on their way, taking the donkey and the great big chattee with them. A little farther on they came to an ants' nest, and the deaf man said to the blind man, "Here are a number of very fine black ants, much larger than any I ever saw before. Let us take some of them home to show to our friends."

"Very well," nodded the blind man. "We will take them as a present to our friends." So the deaf man took a silver snuffbox out of his pocket, and put four or five of the finest black ants into it. They then continued on their journey.

Before they had gone far, a terrible storm came up. It thundered and lightninged and rained and blew with such fury that it seemed as if heaven and earth were at war.

"Oh dear! Oh dear!" cried the deaf man. "How dreadful this lightning is! Let us make haste and get to shelter."

"I don't see that the lightning is dreadful at all," answered the blind man, "but the thunder is very terrible. We must certainly seek some place of shelter."

Not far off they came to a high building, which looked to the deaf man like a fine temple. He and the blind man resolved to spend the night there. They went inside and shut the door, taking the donkey and the big chattee with them.

But this building, which they mistook for a temple, was in truth no temple at all but the house of a powerful Rakshasa, or demon. Hardly had the blind man, the deaf man, and the donkey got inside and fastened the door than the Rakshasa returned home. He found the door fastened and heard people moving about inside.

"Ho! Ho!" he said to himself. "Some men have got in here, have they! I'll soon make mincemeat out of them." So he began to roar in a voice louder than the thunder, and he shouted, "Let me into my house this minute, you wretches! Let me in, let me in, I say!" He kicked the door and battered it with his great fists.

Though the Rakshasa's voice was powerful, his appearance was still more alarming. The deaf man, peeping at him through a chink in the wall, was so frightened that he did not know what to do. But the blind man was brave, because he couldn't see. He went to the door and called out, "Who are you? And what do you mean by battering at the door this way at this time of night?"

"I'm a Rakshasa," answered the Rakshasa angrily, "and this is my house. Let me in this instant, or I'll kill you."

All this time the deaf man, watching the Rakshasa, was shivering and shaking, but the blind man was still very brave and he called out again, "Oh, you're a Rakshasa, are you! Well, if you're Rakshasa, I'm Bakshasa. And Bakshasa is as good as Rakshasa!"

"Bakshasa!" roared the Rakshasa. "Bakshasa! Bakshasa! What nonsense is this? There is no such creature as a Bakshasa!"

"Go away," replied the blind man, "and don't dare to make any further disturbance, lest I punish you. Know that I'm Bakshasa! And Bakshasa is Rakshasa's father!"

"My father?" answered the Rakshasa. "Heaven and earth.

Bakshasa, my father! I never heard anything so extraordinary. You, my father, and in there! I never knew my father was Bakshasa."

"Yes," replied the blind man. "Go away instantly, I command you, for I am your father Bakshasa."

"Very well," answered the Rakshasa, beginning to be puzzled. "But if you're my father, let me first see your face."

The blind man and the deaf man were unsure what they should do now, but at last they opened the door a tiny chink and poked the donkey's nose out.

When the Rakshasa saw this, he thought to himself, "Bless me, what a terribly ugly face my father Bakshasa has!" Then he called out, "O Father Bakshasa, you have a very big, fierce face, but people sometimes have very big heads and very little bodies. Pray let me see your body as well as your head before I go away."

The blind man and the deaf man now rolled the great, big chattee with a thundering noise past the chink in the door.

The Rakshasa, watching attentively, was very surprised when he saw this great black thing rolling along the floor, and he thought, "In truth, my father Bakshasa has a very big body as well as a big head. He's big enough to eat me up altogether. I'd better go away." Still he could not help being a little doubtful, so he cried, "O Bakshasa, Father Bakshasa! You have indeed got a very big head and a very big body. But do, before I go away, let me hear you scream."

The cunning deaf man, seeing what the Rakshasa said,

pulled his silver snuffbox out of his pocket. He took out the black ants, put one in the donkey's right ear, another in the donkey's left ear, and another and another. The ants pinched the poor donkey's ears dreadfully. The donkey was so hurt and frightened that it began to bellow, "Eh augh! Eh augh! Eh augh! Augh! Augh!"

At this terrible noise, the Rakshasa fled in fright, saying, "Enough, enough, Father Bakshasa! The sound of your voice would make the most obstinate Rakshasa obedient."

No sooner had he gone than the deaf man took the ants out of the donkey's ears, and he and the blind man spent the rest of the night in peace and comfort.

Next morning the deaf man woke the blind man early, saying, "Awake, brother, awake. Here we are in great luck. The floor is covered with heaps of gold and silver and precious stones."

"That is a good thing," said the blind man. "Show me where it is so I can help you collect it." They collected as much treasure as they could manage and made four great bundles of it. The blind man took one bundle, the deaf man took another, and putting the other two great bundles on the donkey, they started off home.

However, the Rakshasa whom they had frightened away the night before had not gone very far. He was waiting to see what his father Bakshasa might look like by day. He saw the door of his house open and watched while out walked a blind man, a deaf man, and a donkey, all of them laden with large bundles of his treasure.

The Rakshasa, in a rage, called to six of his friends to help him kill the blind man, the deaf man, and the donkey, and recover the treasure.

The deaf man saw them coming: seven great Rakshasas, with hair a yard long and tusks like an elephant's. He was terrified, but the blind man, still very brave, said, "Brother, why do you lag behind in that way?"

"Oh!" cried the deaf man. "There are seven great Rakshasas with tusks like an elephant's coming to kill us. What can we do?"

"Let us hide the treasure in the bushes," said the blind man, pointing. "And you lead me to a tree. I will climb up first, and you shall climb up afterward. Thus we shall be out of their way." So they pushed the donkey and the bundles of treasure into the bushes, and the deaf man led the blind man to a high tree close by. But he was a very cunning man and instead of letting the blind man climb up first, he got up first and let the blind man follow, so that he was farther out of harm's way than his friend.

When the Rakshasa arrived at the place and saw them both perched out of reach in the tree, he said to his friends, "Let us get on each other's shoulders. We shall then be high enough to pull them down." So one Rakshasa stooped down, and the second got on his shoulders, and the third on his, and the fourth on his, and the fifth on his, and the sixth on his. The seventh and last Rakshasa got on top.

The deaf man became so frightened that he caught hold of his friend's arm, crying, "They're coming, they're coming!" The blind man was not in a very secure position, sitting carelessly at his ease, not knowing how close the Rakshasas were. Thus when the deaf man gave him this unexpected push, he lost his balance and tumbled down onto the neck of the seventh Rakshasa.

The blind man had no idea where he was, but thought he had got onto the branch of some other tree. Stretching out his hand for something to catch hold of, he caught hold of the Rakshasa's two great ears, and pinched them hard in his surprise and fright. With the pain and the weight of the blind man, the Rakshasa lost his balance and fell to the ground, knocking down in turn the sixth, fifth, fourth, third, second, and first Rakshasas, who rolled over one another and lay in a confused heap at the foot of the tree.

Meanwhile the blind man called out to his friend, "Where am I? What has happened? Where am I? Where am I?"

The deaf man, safe up in the tree, called, "Well done, brother! Never fear! Never fear! You're all right, only hold on tight. I'm coming down to help you."

The deaf man had not the least intention of leaving his place of safety, but he continued to call out, "Never mind, brother. Hold on as tight as you can. I'm coming, I'm coming." The more he yelled, the harder the blind man pinched the Rakshasa's ears, which he mistook for palm branches.

The other six Rakshasas, who, after a good deal of kicking, had succeeded in pulling themselves from their tangled heap, had had quite enough of helping their friend, so they ran away as fast as they could.

The seventh Rakshasa thought from their going that the danger must be greater than he knew. Being, moreover, very much afraid of the creature that sat on his shoulders, he put his hands to the back of his ears, and pushed off the blind man. Then, without staying to see who or what it was, he ran after his six companions as fast as he could.

As soon as all the Rakshasas were out of sight, the deaf man came down from the tree and, picking up the blind man, embraced him, saying, "I could not have done better myself. You have frightened away all our enemies." He then dragged the donkey and the bundles of treasure out of the bushes, gave the blind man one bundle to carry, took the second himself, and put the remaining two on the donkey, as before. This done, the whole party set off to return home. But when they had got nearly out of the jungle, the deaf man suggested that they divide the treasure.

"Very well," nodded the blind man. "Divide what we have in the bundles into two equal portions, keeping one half yourself and giving me the other."

The cunning deaf man had no intention of giving up half of the treasure to the blind man. First he took his own bundle of treasure and hid it in the bushes, and then he took the two bundles off the donkey and hid them in the bushes, and he took a good deal of treasure out of the blind man's bundle, which he also hid. Then, taking the small quantity that remained, he divided it into two equal portions, placing half before the blind man and half in front of himself.

When the blind man put out his hand and felt the very little heap of treasure, he became angry and cried, "This is not fair. You are deceiving me. You have kept almost all the treasure for yourself and given me only a very little."

"Oh, oh! How can you be angry?" said the deaf man. "If you do not believe me, feel for yourself. See, my heap of treasure is no larger than yours."

The blind man put out his hands again to feel how much his

friend had kept. When he found that in front of the deaf man lay only a very small heap, no larger than what he had himself received, he got very cross, and said, "Come, come, this won't do. You think you can cheat me in this way because I am blind. But I'm not so stupid as all that. I carried a great bundle of treasure. You carried a great bundle of treasure. And there were two great bundles on the donkey. Do you mean to pretend that all that made no more treasure than these two little heaps? No, indeed. I know better than that."

"Stuff and nonsense!" said the deaf man.

"Stuff or no stuff," continued the other, "you are trying to take me in, and I won't be taken in by you."

And so they went on bickering, scolding, growling, contradicting until the blind man got so enraged that he gave the deaf man a tremendous box on the ear.

The blow was so violent that it made the deaf man hear!

The deaf man, very angry, gave his neighbor in return so hard a blow in the face that it opened the blind man's eyes!

The deaf man could hear as well as see! And the blind man could see as well as hear! This astounded them both so much that they became good friends again. The deaf man confessed to having hidden the bulk of the treasure, which he thereupon dragged forth from its place of concealment, and, having divided it equally, they went home and enjoyed themselves.

The Valiant Chattee-maker

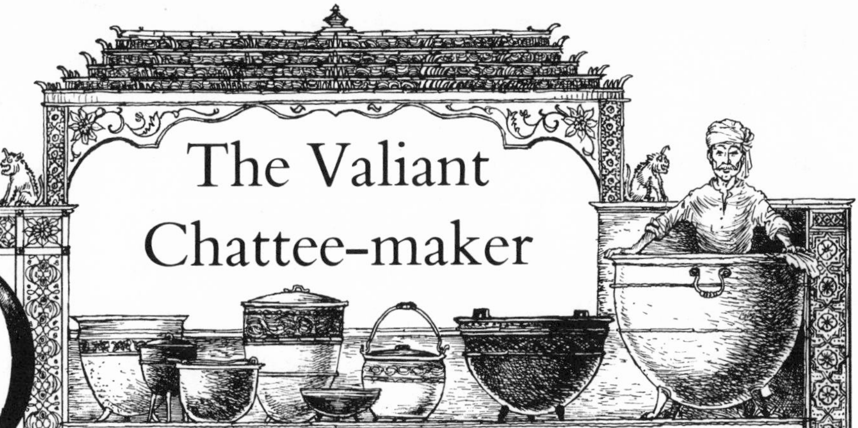

ONCE UPON A TIME, in a violent storm of thunder, lightning, wind, and rain, a tiger crept for shelter close to the wall of an old woman's hut. The old woman was very poor, and her hut but a tumbledown place. Through the roof the rain came drip, drip, drip everywhere. This troubled her so that she ran about from side to side, dragging first one thing and then another from under the leaks in the roof. As she did so she kept saying to herself, "Oh dear! Oh dear! How tiresome this is! I'm sure the roof will come down! If an elephant, or a lion, or a tiger were to walk in, he wouldn't frighten me half so much as does this perpetual dripping." And then she would drag the bed and all the other things in the room about again, to get them out of the way of the dripping water.

The tiger, crouching outside, heard all she said, and thought to himself, "This old woman says she would not be as afraid of an elephant, or a lion, or a tiger as she is of this perpetual dripping. What can this perpetual dripping be? It must be something very dreadful." And hearing her again dragging things about, he said to himself, "What a loud noise! Surely that must be the perpetual dripping."

At this moment a Chattee-maker, a maker of pots, came down the road in search of his straying donkey. The night being cold, he had, truth to say, taken a little more toddy than was good for him, and seeing, by the light of a flash of lightning, a large animal lying close to the old woman's hut, he mistook it for his donkey. Running up to the tiger, he seized it by one ear and began beating, kicking, and abusing it with all his might and main.

"You wretched creature!" he cried. "Is this the way you serve me, obliging me to come out and look for you in pouring rain and on such a dark night as this? Get up instantly, or I'll break every bone in your body." So he went on, scolding and thumping the tiger with all his strength, for he had worked himself up into a terrible rage.

The tiger did not know what to make of it all, but said to himself, "This must be the perpetual dripping. No wonder the old woman said she was more afraid of it than of an elephant, a lion, or a tiger. It gives most dreadfully hard blows."

The Chattee-maker, having made the tiger rise, got on his back and forced the beast to carry him home, kicking and beating the poor animal the whole way, all this time believing he was on his donkey. In front of his house he tied the tiger's forefeet and head together, and fastened him to a post. When he had done this he went to bed.

Next morning, when the Chattee-maker's wife got up and looked out of the window, what did she see but a great big tiger tied to their donkey's post. She was so surprised that she ran to awaken her husband, saying, "Do you know what animal you fetched home last night?"

"The donkey, to be sure," he answered.

"Come and look," said she, and she showed him the great tiger tied to the post. At this the Chattee-maker was no less astonished than his wife. He felt himself all over to see if the tiger had wounded him. No, he was safe and sound; and there was the tiger still fastened to the post.

News of the Chattee-maker's exploit soon spread through the village, and everyone came to see him and hear him tell how he had caught the tiger and tied it to a post. This they thought so wonderful that they sent a deputation to the Rajah with a letter telling him how a man of their village, alone and unarmed, had caught a great tiger and tied it to a post.

When the Rajah read the letter he also was surprised. He determined to go in person to see so astonishing a sight. He sent for his horses and carriages, his lords and attendants, and off they all went to look at the Chattee-maker and the tiger he had caught.

Now the tiger was a very large one, and had long been the terror of the country around, which made the whole matter still more extraordinary. The Rajah decided to bestow all possible honor on the valiant Chattee-maker. He gave him houses and lands, and as much money as would fill a well.

He made him a lord in his court, and conferred on him the command of ten thousand horses.

It came to pass, shortly after this, that a neighboring Rajah, who had long had a quarrel with this one, announced his intention to go to war with him. It was learned that this foreign Rajah had gathered a great army on the borders, and was prepared to invade the country.

No one knew what to do. The Rajah inquired of all his generals which one would be willing to take command of his forces to oppose the enemy. They all replied that the country was too ill-prepared. The cause was so hopeless that they did not wish to take the responsibility of chief command. The Rajah did not know whom he could appoint until some of his people said, "You have lately given the command of ten thousand horses to the valiant Chattee-maker who caught the tiger. Why not make him commander in chief? A man who could catch a tiger and tie him to a post must surely be more courageous and clever than most."

"Very well," said the Rajah, "I will make him commander in chief." So he sent for the Chattee-maker and said to him, "In your hands I place all the power of the kingdom. You must put our enemies to flight."

"So be it," answered the Chattee-maker. "But before I lead the whole army against the enemy, allow me to go by myself and examine their position and, if possible, find out their numbers and strength."

The Rajah consented. The Chattee-maker returned home and said to his wife, "The Rajah has made me commander in

chief of his forces. It is a very difficult post for me to fill, because I shall have to ride at the head of the army, and you know that I have never in my life been on a horse. But I have succeeded in gaining a little delay. The Rajah has given me permission to go first alone and examine the enemy's camp. Get me a very quiet pony, for you know I cannot ride, and I will start tomorrow morning."

But before the Chattee-maker left, the Rajah sent over a most magnificent charger richly bedecked for him to ride when going to see the enemy's camp.

The Chattee-maker was frightened indeed, for this great steed was powerful and spirited. He felt sure that even if he were able to get on it, he would very soon tumble off. But he did not dare to refuse it, lest he offend the Rajah. So he sent back to him a message of thanks, and said to his wife, "I cannot go on the pony, now that the Rajah has sent me this fine horse; but however am I to ride it?"

"Oh, don't be frightened," she answered. "You've only got to get up on it. I will tie you on firmly, so that you cannot tumble off. If you start at night, no one will see that you are tied on."

"Very well," he replied.

That night the Chattee-maker's wife brought to the door the horse that the Rajah had sent. "Indeed," said the Chattee-maker, "I can never get into that saddle. It is so high up."

"You must jump," said his wife. So several times the Chattee-maker tried to jump, but each time he tumbled down again. "I always forget when I am jumping," said he, "which way I ought to turn."

"Your face must be toward the horse's head," she answered.

"To be sure, of course!" he cried, and giving one great leap he jumped into the saddle, but with his face toward the horse's tail.

"This won't do at all," said his wife as she helped him down again. "Try getting on without jumping."

"I never can remember," he said, "when I have got my left foot in the stirrup, what to do with my right foot or where to put it."

"That must go in the other stirrup," she answered. "Let me help you."

Since the horse was fresh and lively and did not like standing still, it took many trials and many tumbles before the Chattee-maker got into the saddle. And no sooner had he got there than he cried, "Oh, wife, wife! Tie me very firmly as quickly as possible, for I know I shall jump down if I can."

The Chattee-maker's wife quickly fetched some strong rope and tied his feet firmly into the stirrups. She fastened one stirrup to the other, and put another rope round his waist and another round his neck, and fastened them all to the horse's body and neck and tail.

When the horse felt all these ropes about him, he could not imagine what queer creature had got upon his back, and he began rearing and kicking and prancing. At last he set off at full gallop, as fast as he could tear, right across country.

"Wife, wife!" cried the Chattee-maker. "You forgot to tie my hands."

"Hold on by the mane!" she shouted after him. So he caught hold of the horse's mane as firmly as he could. Then away went horse, away went Chattee-maker – away, away, away, over hedges, over ditches, over rivers, over plains – away, away, like a flash of lightning – now this way, now that – on, on, on, gallop, gallop, gallop – until they came in sight of the enemy's camp.

The Chattee-maker did not like his ride at all, and when he saw where it was leading him he liked it still less, for he thought the enemy would catch him and very likely kill him. He determined to make one desperate effort to be free. He stretched out his hand and seized a large banyan tree as he galloped past. He held on with all his might, hoping that this action would cause his ropes to break. But the horse was going so fast, and the soil in which the banyan tree grew was so loose, that when the Chattee-maker caught hold of the tree and gave it a violent pull, it came up by the roots, and on he rode as fast as before, with the tree in his hand.

All the soldiers in the camp saw him coming. Having heard that an army was to be sent against them, they imagined that the Chattee-maker was the one in the lead. "See," they cried, "here comes a man of gigantic stature on a mighty horse! He is one of the enemy. The whole army must be close at hand. If they are such as he, we are all dead men."

Running to their Rajah, the soldiers cried, "Here comes the whole force of the enemy. They are men of gigantic stature, mounted on mighty horses. As they come, they tear up the very trees in their rage. We can oppose men, but not such monsters as these." Other soldiers followed and said, "It is true," for by this time the Chattee-maker had got near the camp. "They are coming! They are coming! Let us fly! Let us fly! Fly! Fly, for your lives!"

The panic-stricken multitude fled from the camp. They had their Rajah write a letter to the one whose country he was about to invade to say that he would not do so, and to propose peace.

Scarcely had everyone fled from the camp when the horse on which the Chattee-maker rode came galloping into it. The Chattee-maker was almost dead from fatigue, but the banyan tree was still in his hand. Just as he reached the camp the ropes by which he was tied broke and let him fall to the ground. The horse stood still, too tired with his long run to go farther.

On recovering his senses, the Chattee-maker found to his

surprise that the whole camp, full of rich arms, clothes, and trappings, was entirely deserted. In the royal tent, moreover, he found a letter addressed to his Rajah, announcing the retreat of the invading army and proposing terms of peace.

The Chattee-maker took the letter and returned home with it as fast as he could, leading his horse all the way, for he was afraid to mount him again. By the direct road he reached home just before nightfall. His wife ran out to meet him, overjoyed at his speedy return. As soon as he saw her, he said, "Ah, wife, since last I saw you I've been all around the world, and had many wonderful and terrible adventures. But never mind that now. Send this letter quickly to the Rajah, and the horse also. Since the horse looks so tired, the Rajah will see what a long ride I've had. By sending it ahead, I shall not be obliged to ride it up to the palace tomorrow morning and most likely tumble off."

The next day the Chattee-maker went to the palace. When the people saw him, they cried, "This man is as modest as he is brave. After putting our enemies to flight, he walks quite simply to the door instead of riding here in state as another man would."

The Rajah came to the palace door to meet the Chattee-maker, and paid him all possible honor. Terms of peace were agreed upon between the two countries, and the Chattee-maker was rewarded for all he had done with twice as much rank and wealth as he had had before. And he lived very happily all the rest of his life.

Ireland

The Bee, the Harp, the Mouse, and the Bum-clock

ONCE A WIDOW had one son, called Jack. Jack and his mother owned just three cows. They lived well and were happy for a long time, but at last hard times came down on them. Their crops failed, and poverty looked in at the door. Indeed, things got so bad for the widow she had to make up her mind to sell one of their three cows.

"Jack," she said one night, "in the morning you must go to the fair to sell the branny cow."

In the morning brave Jack was up early. He took a stick in his fist and turned out the cow, and off he went with her.

When Jack came to the fair, he saw a great crowd gathered in a ring in the street. He went into the crowd to see what they were looking at. There in the middle of them he saw a man with a wee, wee harp, a mouse, and a cockroach, which is called a bum-clock, and a bee to play on the harp.

When the man put them down on the ground and whistled, the bee began to play the harp. The mouse and the bum-clock stood up on their hind legs and got hold of each other and began to waltz. And as soon as the harp began to play and the mouse and the bum-clock to dance, there wasn't a man or a woman, or a thing in the fair, that didn't begin to dance also. The pots and pans and the wheels and reels jumped and jigged all over the town, and Jack himself and the branny cow as much as the next. There was never a town in such a state before or since.

After a while the man picked up the bee, the harp, the mouse, and the bum-clock and put them into his pocket. The men and women, Jack and the cow, the pots and pans, the wheels and reels that had hopped and jigged now stopped, and everyone began to laugh as if to break his heart.

The man turned to Jack. "Jack," said he, "how would you like to be master of all these animals?"

"Why," said Jack, "I should like it fine."

"Well, then," said the man, "how will we make a bargain about them?"

"I have no money," said Jack.

"But you have a fine cow," said the man. "I will give you the bee and the harp for it."

"Oh, but," Jack said, said he, "my poor mother at home is very sad entirely. I have this cow to sell and lift her heart again."

"And better than this she cannot get," said the man. "For when she sees the bee play the harp, she will laugh if she never laughed in her life before."

"Well," said Jack, said he, "that will be grand."

He made the bargain. The man took the cow, and Jack started home with the bee and the harp in his pocket. When he came home, his mother welcomed him back.

"And Jack," said she, "I see you have sold the cow."

"I have done that," said Jack.

"Did you do well?" said the mother.

"I did well, and very well," said Jack.

"How much did you get for her?" said the mother.

"Oh," said he, "it was not for money at all I sold her, but for something far better."

"Oh, Jack! Jack!" said she. "What have you done?"

"Just wait until you see, Mother," said he, "and you will soon say I have done well."

Out of his pocket he took the bee and the harp and set them in the middle of the floor and whistled to them. As soon as he did this the bee began to play the harp. The mother she looked at them and let a big, great laugh out of her, and she and Jack began dancing and jigging. The pots and pans, the wheels and reels also began to dance and jig over the floor. And the house itself hopped about, too.

When Jack picked up the bee and the harp again, the dancing all stopped, and his mother she laughed for a long time. But when she came to herself, she got very angry entirely with Jack, and she told him he was a silly, foolish fellow. There was neither food nor money in the house, and now he had lost one of her good cows, also.

"We must do something to live," said she. "Over to the fair you must go tomorrow morning and take the black cow with you and sell her."

Off in the morning at an early hour brave Jack started, and never halted until he was in the fair.

When he came into the fair, he saw a big crowd gathered in a ring in the street. Said Jack to himself, "I wonder what they are looking at." Into the crowd he pushed, and saw the wee man this day again with a mouse and a bum-clock.

When the man put them down in the street and whistled, the mouse and the bum-clock stood up on their hind legs and got hold of each other. They began to dance there and jig. As they did, there was not a man or woman in the street who didn't begin to jig also. Jack and the black cow, the wheels and the reels, and the pots and pans – all of them were jigging and dancing all over the town. And the houses themselves were jumping and hopping about, too. Such a place Jack or anyone else never saw before.

When the man lifted the mouse and the bum-clock into his pocket, they all stopped dancing and settled down.

The man turned to Jack. "Jack," said he, "I am glad to see you. How would you like to have these animals?"

"I should like well to have them," said Jack, said he, "only I cannot."

"Why cannot you?" asked the man.

"Oh," said Jack, said he, "I have no money, and my poor mother is very downhearted. She sent me to the fair to sell this cow and bring some money to lift her heart."

"Oh," said the man, said he, "if you want to lift your mother's heart, I will sell you the mouse. When you set the bee to play the harp and the mouse to dance to it, your mother will laugh if she never laughed in her life before."

"But I have no money," said Jack, said he, "to buy your mouse."

"I don't mind," said the man, said he, "I will take your cow for it."

Poor Jack was so taken with the mouse and had his mind so set on it that he thought it was a grand bargain entirely. He gave the man his cow, and took the mouse and started off for home. When he got home his mother welcomed him.

"Jack," said she, "I see you have sold the cow."

"I did that," said Jack.

"Did you sell her well?" asked she.

"Very well indeed," said Jack, said he.

"How much did you get for her?"

"I didn't get money," said he, "but something far better."

"Oh, Jack! Jack!" said she. "What do you mean?"

"I will soon show you that, Mother," said he, taking the mouse out of his pocket, and the harp and the bee, and setting them all on the floor. When he began to whistle, the bee began to play, and the mouse got up on its hind legs and began to dance and jig. The mother gave such a hearty laugh as she never laughed in her life before. And she and Jack began dancing and jigging. The pots and pans and wheels and reels also began to dance and jig over the floor. And the house itself hopped all about, too.

When they were tired of this, Jack lifted the harp and the mouse and the bee and put them in his pocket, and his mother she laughed for a long time.

But when she came to herself, she got very angry entirely with Jack.

"Oh, Jack!" she said. "You are a stupid, good-for-nothing fellow. We have neither money nor meat in the house, and here you have lost two of my good cows, and I have only one left now. Tomorrow morning," she said, "you must be up early and take this cow to the fair and sell her. See you get something this time to lift my heart up."

"I will do that," said Jack, said he. And so he went to his bed.

Early in the morning Jack was up and turned out the spotty cow, and went again to the fair.

When Jack came into the fair, he saw a crowd gathered in a ring in the street. "I wonder what they are looking at, anyhow," said he. He pushed through the crowd, and there he saw the same wee man he had seen before, with a bum-clock.

When the man put the bum-clock on the ground, he whistled, and the bum-clock began to dance. And as soon as the bum-clock began to dance, the men, women, and children in the street, and Jack and the spotty cow began to dance and jig also. Everything on the street and about it, the wheels and reels, the pots and pans, began to jig. And the houses themselves began to dance likewise.

When the man lifted the bum-clock and put it in his pocket, everybody stopped jigging and dancing and laughed loud. The wee man turned and saw Jack.

"Jack, my brave boy," said he, "you will never be right-fixed until you have this bum-clock, for it is a very fancy thing to have."

"Oh, but," said Jack, said he, "I have no money."

"No matter for that," said the man, "you have a cow, and that is as good as money to me."

"Well," said Jack, "I have a poor mother who is very down-hearted at home. She sent me to the fair to sell this cow and raise some money and lift her heart."

"Oh, but Jack," said the wee man, "this bum-clock is the very thing to lift her heart. When you put down your harp and bee and mouse on the floor, and put the bum-clock along with them, she will laugh if she never laughed in her life before."

"Well, that is surely true," said Jack, said he, "and I think I will make a swap with you."

So Jack gave the cow to the man, and took the bum-clock himself, and started for home. His mother was glad to see Jack back.

"And Jack," said she, "I see that you have sold the cow."

"I did that, Mother."

"Did you sell her well, Jack?" said his mother.

"Very well indeed, Mother," said Jack.

"How much did you get for her?" said his mother.

"I didn't take any money for her, Mother, but something

far better," said Jack. He took out of his pocket the bum-clock and the mouse, and the bee and the harp, and set them on the floor and began to whistle. The bee began to play the harp, and the mouse and the bum-clock stood up on their hind legs and began to dance, and Jack's mother laughed very heartily. Everything in the house, the wheels and the reels and the pots and pans, went jigging and hopping over the floor. And the house itself went jigging and hopping about likewise.

When Jack lifted up the animals and put them in his pocket, everything stopped, and the mother laughed for a good while. But after a bit, when she came to herself, she saw what Jack had done and how they were without money, or food, or a cow. She got very, very angry at Jack. She scolded him hard and then sat down and began to cry.

Poor Jack, when he looked at himself, confessed that he was a stupid fool entirely.

"And what," said he, "shall I now do for my poor mother?"

One day soon, Jack went out along the road, thinking and thinking, and he met a wee woman who said, "Good morrow to you, Jack. How is it you are not trying for the daughter of the King of Ireland?"

"What do you mean?" said Jack.

Said she, "Didn't you hear what the whole world has heard, that the King of Ireland has a daughter who hasn't laughed for seven years? He has promised to give her in marriage, and to give the kingdom along with her, to any man who will take three laughs out of her."

"If that is so," said Jack, said he, "it is not here I should be."

Back to the house he went, and gathered together the bee, the harp, the mouse, and the bum-clock. Putting them into his pocket, he bade his mother good-bye. He told her it wouldn't be long till she got good news from him, and off he hurried.

When Jack reached the castle, there was a ring of spikes all around and men's heads on nearly every spike there.

"What heads are these?" Jack asked one of the King's soldiers.

"Any man that comes here trying to win the King's daughter, and fails to make her laugh three times, he loses his head and has it stuck on a spike. These are the heads of the men that failed," said he.

"A mighty big crowd," said Jack, said he. Then Jack sent word to tell the King's daughter and the King that there was a new man who had come to win her.

In a very little time, the King and the King's daughter and

the King's Court all came out. They sat themselves down on gold and silver chairs in front of the castle and ordered Jack to be brought in until he should have his trial.

Jack, before he went, took out of his pocket the bee, the harp, the mouse, and the bum-clock. He gave the harp to the bee, and he tied a string to one and the other. He took the end of the string himself and marched into the castle yard before all the Court, with his animals coming on a string behind him.

When the Queen and the King and the Court saw poor ragged Jack with his bee, his mouse, and with his bum-clock hopping behind him on a string, they set up one roar of laughter that was long and loud enough. And when the King's daughter herself lifted her head to see what they were laughing at, and saw Jack and his menagerie, she opened her mouth and she let out of her such a laugh as was never heard before.

Jack made a low bow, and said, "Thank you, my lady. You have given me one of the three laughs."

Then he drew up his animals in a circle and began to whistle. The minute he did so, the bee began to play the harp. The mouse and the bum-clock stood up on their hind legs, got hold of each other, and began to dance. The King and the King's Court and Jack himself began to dance and jig, and everything about the King's castle – pots and pans, wheels and reels, and the castle itself – began to dance also. And the King's daughter, when she saw this, opened her mouth again. She let out of her a laugh twice louder than she let before.

Jack, in the middle of his jigging, made another bow, and

said, "Thank you, my lady. You have given me two of the three laughs."

Jack and his animals went on playing and dancing. But Jack could not get the third laugh out of the King's daughter, and the poor lad saw his big head in danger of going on the spike.

Then the brave mouse came to Jack's help and wheeled around upon its heel. As it did so, its tail swiped into the bum-clock's mouth, and the bum-clock began to cough and cough and cough.

When the King's daughter saw this, she opened her mouth again, and she let out the loudest and hardest and merriest laugh that was ever heard before or since.

"Thank you, my lady," said Jack, making another bow. "I have all of you won."

When Jack stopped his animals, the King took him and the animals within the castle. Jack was washed and combed. He was dressed in a suit of silk and satin, with all kinds of gold and silver ornaments, and then was led before the King's daughter. And true enough, she confessed that a handsomer and finer fellow than Jack she had never seen. She was very willing to be his wife.

Jack sent for his poor old mother and brought her to the wedding, which lasted nine days and nine nights, and every night was better than the other.

Billy Beg and the Bull

ONCE UPON A TIME when pigs were swine, a King and a Queen had one son and he was called Billy Beg. Now, the Queen gave Billy a bull that he was very fond of, and it was just as fond of him. But after some time the Queen died. Her last request to the King had been that he would never part Billy and his bull, and the King promised that come what might, come what may, he would not.

Soon the King married again. The new Queen didn't take to Billy Beg, and no more did she like the bull, seeing himself and Billy so friendly. No way could she get the King to part Billy and the bull, so she asked a henwife what she could do.

"And what will you give me," asked the henwife, "if I very soon part them?"

"Whatever you ask," said the Queen.

"Well and good then," said the henwife. "You are to take to your bed. You must pretend that you are bad with a complaint, and I'll do the rest of it."

The Queen took to her bed and none of the doctors could do anything for her. So the Queen asked for the henwife. When she came and examined the Queen, she said there was one thing, and only one, could cure her.

The King asked what was that. The henwife said it was three mouthfuls of the blood of Billy Beg's bull. But the King wouldn't hear of this.

The next day the Queen was worse. The third day she was worse still. She told the King she was dying, and he'd have her death on his head. So, at last, the King had to consent to the killing of Billy Beg's bull.

When Billy heard this, he got very down in the heart entirely. The bull saw him looking so mournful, and asked what was wrong with him. So Billy told the bull what was wrong. The bull told him never to mind, but to keep up his heart. The Queen would never taste a drop of his blood.

The next day, when the bull was led up to be killed, said he to Billy, "Jump up on my back till we see what kind of a horseman you are."

Up Billy jumped on his back. With that the bull leaped nine miles high, nine miles deep, and nine miles broad, and came down with Billy sticking between his horns.

Hundreds were looking on dazed at the sight, and through them the bull rushed, right over the Queen, killing her dead.

Away the bull galloped, over high hills and low, over the Cove of Cork and old Tom Fox with his bugle horn.

At last they stopped. "Now, then," said the bull to Billy, "put your hand in my left ear, and you'll find a napkin. When you spread it out, it will be covered with food and drink of all sorts, fit for the King himself."

Billy did this, and then he spread out the napkin. He ate and drank to his heart's content, then he rolled the napkin and put it back in the bull's ear.

"And now," said the bull, "put your hand into my right ear and you'll find a bit of a stick. If you wind it over your head three times, it will turn into a sword and give you the strength of a thousand men besides your own. When you have no more need of it as a sword, it will change back into a stick again."

Billy did all this. "Well and good," said the bull. "At twelve o'clock tomorrow, I'll have to meet and fight a great bull."

Billy got up again on the bull's back. The bull started off and away, over high hills and low, over the Cove of Cork and old Tom Fox with his bugle horn.

There they stopped and Billy's bull met the other bull. Both of them fought, and the like of their fight was never seen before or since. They knocked the soft ground into hard, and the hard into soft, the soft into spring wells, the spring wells into rocks, and the rocks into high hills. They fought long, and Billy Beg's bull killed the other and drank his blood.

Billy took the napkin out of the bull's ear again. He spread it out and ate a hearty dinner.

Then said the bull to Billy, said he, "At twelve o'clock tomorrow, I'm to meet the brother of the bull I killed today, and we'll have a hard fight."

Billy got on the bull's back again, and the bull started off, over high hills and low, over the Cove of Cork and old Tom Fox with his bugle horn.

Here he met the bull's brother, and they set to and fought long and hard. At last Billy's bull killed the other and drank his blood.

Again, Billy took the napkin out of the bull's ear and spread it out and ate a hearty dinner.

Now said the bull to Billy, said he, "Tomorrow at twelve o'clock I'm to fight the brother of the two bulls I killed. He's a mighty bull entirely, the strongest of them all. He's called the Black Bull of the Forest, and he'll be too much for me.

"When I'm dead," said the bull, "you, Billy, will take with you the napkin, and you'll never be hungry; and the stick, and you'll be able to overcome everything that gets in your way. And take out your knife and cut a strip off my hide and make a belt of it. As long as you wear this belt, you cannot be killed."

Billy was very sorry to hear this. But he got up on the bull's back again, and they started off.

Sure enough, at twelve o'clock the next day, they met the great Black Bull of the Forest. Both of the bulls began to fight, and they fought hard and long. But at last the Black Bull of the Forest killed Billy Beg's bull and drank his blood.

Billy Beg was so sad at this that for two days he sat over the bull. He neither ate nor drank, but cried salt tears all the time.

After the two days, Billy got up. He spread out the napkin and ate a hearty dinner, for he was very hungry now. Then he cut a strip off the hide of the bull and made a belt for himself.

Taking it and the bit of stick and the napkin, he set out to push his fortune.

Well, now, Billy traveled for three days and three nights until at last he came to a great gentleman's place. He asked the gentleman if he could give him work, and the man said he wanted just such a boy as him for herding cattle.

Billy asked what cattle would he have to herd and what wages would he get.

The gentleman said he had three goats, three cows, three horses, and three donkeys that he fed in an orchard. Also, he said that no boy who went with them ever came back alive, for there were three giants – and these were brothers – that came to milk the cows and the goats every day. Always they killed the boy that was herding. If Billy wished to try, he could, but they wouldn't fix his wages until they'd see if he would come back alive.

"Agreed, then," said Billy.

The next morning Billy got up and drove the animals to the orchard and began to feed them. About the middle of the day he heard three terrible roars that shook the apples off the trees, shook the horns on the cows, and made the hair stand up on Billy's head.

In came a frightful big giant with three heads and began to threaten Billy. "You're too big for one bite, and too small for two," bellowed the giant. "What will I do with you?"

"I'll fight you," answered Billy, stepping out to him and swinging the bit of stick three times over his head. The stick changed into a sword and gave him the strength of a thousand men besides his own.

But the giant laughed at the size of him. "Well, how will I kill you?" asked he. "Will it be by a swing by the back or a cut of the sword?"

"With a swing by the back," said Billy, "if you can."

They both laid hold for a wrestle, and Billy lifted the giant clean off the ground.

"Oh, have mercy," said the giant. But Billy took up his sword and killed the giant then and there.

It was evening by this time, so Billy drove home the three goats, three cows, three horses, and three donkeys. That night all the dishes in the house could not hold the milk the cows had to give.

"Well," said the gentleman, "this beats me. I never saw anyone coming back alive out of there before, nor the cows with a drop of milk. Did you see anything in the orchard?" asked he.

"Nothing worse than myself," said Billy. "And what about my wages now?"

"Well," said the gentleman, "you'll hardly come alive out of the orchard tomorrow. So we'll wait until after that."

Next morning his master told Billy that something must have happened to one of the giants. He used to hear the cries of three giants every night, but last night he only heard two crying.

That morning, after Billy had eaten breakfast, he drove the animals into the orchard again, and began to feed them.

About twelve o'clock he heard three terrible roars that shook the apples off the trees, the horns on the cows, and made the hair stand up on Billy's head. In came a frightful big giant with six heads. He told Billy he would make him pay for killing his brother yesterday. "You're too big for one bite and too small for two. What will I do with you?" bellowed the giant.

Well, the long and the short of it is that Billy lifted this giant clean off the ground, too, and took up his sword and killed him then and there.

It was evening by this time, so Billy drove the animals home again. The milk the cows gave that night overflowed all the dishes in the house, and, running out, turned a rusty mill that hadn't been turned for thirty years.

If the master was surprised to see Billy come back the night before, he was ten times more surprised now. "Did you see anything in the orchard today?"

"Nothing worse than myself," said Billy. "And what about my wages now?"

"Well, never mind about your wages till tomorrow," said the gentleman. "I think you'll hardly come back alive again."

Billy went to his bed, and the gentleman went to his.

When the gentleman rose in the morning, said he to Billy, "I don't know what's wrong with two of the giants. Only one did I hear crying last night."

Well, when Billy had eaten his breakfast, he set out to the orchard once more, driving before him the animals.

Sure enough, about the middle of the day he heard three terrible roars again. In came another giant, this one with twelve heads on him.

"You villain, you," thundered the giant. "You killed my two brothers, and I'll have my revenge on you now. But you're too big for one bite and too small for two. What will I do with you?"

Again it ended with brave Billy lifting the giant clean off the ground and taking his sword and killing him.

That evening Billy drove his animals home. This time the milk of the cows had to be turned into a valley, where it made a lake three miles long and three miles broad and three miles deep.

Now the gentleman wondered more than ever to find Billy back alive. "Did you see nothing in the orchard today, Billy?" he asked.

"No, nothing worse than myself," said Billy.

"Well, that beats me," said the gentleman.

"What about my wages now?" asked Billy.

"Well, you're a good mindful boy," said the gentleman, "and I'll give you any wages you ask for the future."

The next morning the gentleman said to Billy, "Not one giant did I hear crying last night. I don't know what has happened to them."

That day the gentleman said to Billy, "Now you must look after the cattle again, Billy, while I go to see the fight."

"What fight?" asked Billy.

"Why," said the gentleman, "the King's daughter is going to be eaten by a fiery dragon, if the greatest fighter in the land doesn't kill the dragon first. And if he's able to kill the dragon, the King is to give him his daughter in marriage."

"That will be fine," said Billy.

Billy drove the animals to the orchard again, and the like of all the people that passed by that day to see the fight, he had never seen before. They went in coaches and carriages, on horses and donkeys, riding and walking, crawling and creeping. Said one man that was passing, to Billy, "Why don't you come to see the great fight?"

"What would take the likes of me there?" said Billy.

But when Billy found them all gone, he saddled and bridled the best black horse his master had. He put on the best suit of clothes he could get in his master's house and rode off to the fight after the rest.

When he arrived, he saw the King's daughter with the

whole court about her on a platform before the castle. He had never before seen anything half so beautiful.

The great warrior that was to fight the dragon was walking up and down on the lawn before her, with three men carrying his sword. And everyone in the whole country was gathered there looking at him.

But when the fiery dragon came up, with twelve heads on him and every mouth spitting fire, and let twelve roars out of him, the warrior ran away and hid himself up to the neck in a well of water. No one could get him to come and face the dragon.

The King's daughter asked then if there was no one there to save her from the dragon. But no one stirred.

When Billy saw this, he tied the belt of the bull's hide around him, swung his stick over his head, and went in.

After a terrible fight entirely, he killed the dragon. And then everyone gathered about to find out who the stranger was. But Billy jumped on his horse and darted away sooner than let them know. Only, just as he was getting away, the King's daughter pulled the shoe off his foot.

Now, when the dragon was killed, the warrior that had hid in the well came out. He brought the dragon's heads to the King, and said that it was he in disguise who had killed the dragon.

But the King's daughter tried the shoe on him and found it didn't fit. And she said she would marry no one but the man the shoe fitted.

When Billy got home he quickly took off the fine suit, and

he had the horse in the stable and the cattle all home before his master returned.

When the master came, he began telling Billy about the wonderful day they had had entirely. He told about the grand stranger that came riding down out of a cloud on a black horse and killed the fiery dragon and then vanished in a cloud again.

"Now, Billy," said he, "wasn't that wonderful?"

"It was, indeed," said Billy, "very wonderful entirely."

After that it was announced over the country that all the people were to come to the King's castle on a certain day, so that the King's daughter could try the shoe on them. The one it fitted, she was to marry.

When the day arrived, Billy was in the orchard with the three goats, three cows, three horses, and three donkeys, as usual.

The like of all the crowds that passed that day going to the King's castle to try on the shoe, he had never seen before. They all asked Billy if he was not going to the King's castle, but Billy said, "Now, what would be bringing the likes of me there?"

At last when all the others had gone, there passed an old man wearing a scarecrow suit of rags. Billy stopped him and asked what he would take to swap clothes with him.

"Now, don't be playing off your jokes on my clothes," said the old man, "or maybe I'll be making you feel my stick."

But Billy soon let him see it was in earnest he was, and both of them swapped suits. Billy, however, did not give up his belt.

Off to the castle started Billy, with the suit of rags on his back and an old stick in his hand. When he got there, he found everyone in great commotion trying on the shoe. Some of them were cutting down a foot, trying to get it to fit. But it was all of no use: the shoe would fit none.

The King's daughter was about to give up in despair, when a ragged-looking boy, which was Billy, elbowed his way through and asked, "Let me try it on; maybe it would fit me."

But the people all began to laugh at the sight of him. "Go along," said they, shoving and pushing him back.

But the King's daughter saw him and called out to let him come and try on the shoe.

So Billy went up, and all the people looked on, breaking their hearts with laughing. But what would you have of it—the shoe fitted Billy as nice as if it were made on his foot! And so the King's daughter claimed Billy as her husband. He confessed it was he that had killed the fiery dragon.

When the King had Billy dressed up in a silk and satin suit, with plenty of gold and silver on it, everyone gave in that his like they had never seen before.

Billy was married to the King's daughter, and the wedding lasted nine days, nine hours, nine minutes, nine half minutes, and nine quarter minutes; and they lived happy and well from that day to this.

Italy

Cenerentola

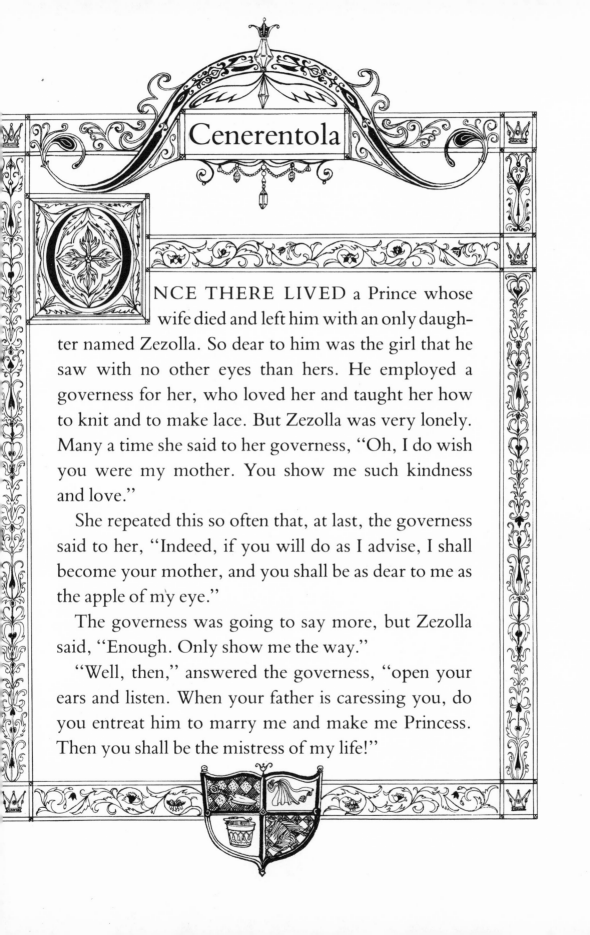

ONCE THERE LIVED a Prince whose wife died and left him with an only daughter named Zezolla. So dear to him was the girl that he saw with no other eyes than hers. He employed a governess for her, who loved her and taught her how to knit and to make lace. But Zezolla was very lonely. Many a time she said to her governess, "Oh, I do wish you were my mother. You show me such kindness and love."

She repeated this so often that, at last, the governess said to her, "Indeed, if you will do as I advise, I shall become your mother, and you shall be as dear to me as the apple of my eye."

The governess was going to say more, but Zezolla said, "Enough. Only show me the way."

"Well, then," answered the governess, "open your ears and listen. When your father is caressing you, do you entreat him to marry me and make me Princess. Then you shall be the mistress of my life!"

After Zezolla heard this, each hour seemed a thousand years long until she was able to do as her governess advised. When the mourning for her mother was ended, Zezolla began to beg her father to marry her governess. At first the Prince took it only lightly, but Zezolla went on until he gave way. He married the governess, then, and gave a great feast at the wedding.

Now, while the young people were dancing, and Zezolla was standing at the window, a dove flew over and perched on the wall. It said to her, "Whenever you need anything, send your request to the Dove of the Fairies in the Island of Sardinia, and instantly you will have what you desire."

For five or six days, the new stepmother nearly smothered Zezolla with affection. She gave her choice morsels to eat and clothed her in rich dresses. But before long, she brought forward six daughters of her own, though she had never told anyone that she was a widow with all these girls. She began to praise them and to talk about them to the Prince in such a way that at last the stepdaughters had won all his favor. Thoughts of Zezolla, his own child, went right out of his heart. In short, it began to go so ill with the poor girl that she was sent from the royal chamber down to the kitchen, and even her name was changed. Instead of Zezolla, she was called Cenerentola, which in another language means Cinderella.

One day it happened that the Prince had to go to Sardinia on affairs of state. Calling to him the six stepdaughters, he asked them, one by one, what they would like him to bring them on his return. One wished for beautiful dresses, another to have some head ornaments, another rouge for the face, another toys and trinkets – one wished for this and another for that. At last the Prince turned to his own daughter and asked, as if in mockery, "And what would you have, child?"

"Nothing, Father," Cenerentola replied. "But commend me to the Dove of the Fairies, and bid her send me something. And if you forget my request, may you be unable to stir backwards or forwards. Remember what I tell you, for it will fare with you accordingly."

The Prince then went on his way and took care of his business in Sardinia. He procured all the things his stepdaughters had asked for, but he quite forgot Cenerentola. When he boarded his ship to return, the ship could not get out of the harbor. It stuck there fast, as if held by a sea creature. The captain of the ship, who was tired out and almost in despair, laid himself down to sleep. In his dream he saw a fairy, who asked him, "Know you not the reason why you cannot sail the ship out of port? It is because the Prince who is on board has broken his promise to his daughter."

The captain awoke and told his dream to the Prince, who in shame and confusion went at once to the Grotto of the Fairies. He commended his daughter to them and asked them to send her something. At once there stepped forth from the grotto a beautiful maiden, who told him that she thanked his daughter for her kind remembrances. She bade him tell her to be merry and of good heart. She gave him a date tree, a golden hoe with which to hoe it, a small golden bucket with which to water it, and a silken napkin with which to wipe its leaves.

The Prince, marveling at all this, took leave of the fairy. He was now able to sail away and return to his own country. After he had presented his stepdaughters with all the things they had asked for, he gave his own daughter her gifts from the fairy. Cenerentola, overjoyed, planted the date tree in a pretty pot; she hoed the earth around it, watered it, and wiped its leaves morning and evening with the silken napkin.

In a few days the tree had grown as tall as a woman. And out of it stepped a fairy, who asked Cenerentola, "What is your wish?"

Cenerentola answered that she wished sometimes to leave the house without her sisters' knowing it.

The fairy quickly answered, "Whenever you desire this, come to the flower pot and say:

'My little date tree, my golden tree,
With a golden hoe I have hoed thee,
With a golden can I have watered thee,
With a silken cloth I have wiped thee dry,
Now strip thee and dress me speedily.'

And when you wish to remove your new garments, change the last words and say, *'Strip me and dress thee.'* "

Soon there came the eve of a great feast. The stepsisters appeared bedecked elegantly, in ribbons and flowers, slippers and bells. It made Cenerentola run to the flower pot to repeat the words the fairy had given her. At once she found herself arrayed like a queen, far more splendid than her stepsisters. She was seated upon a fine horse and attended by twelve smart pages, all in bright raiment.

Off Cenerentola rode to the ball, where she made the sisters envious of an unknown beauty. The young King himself attended the ball, and as soon as he saw Cenerentola, he stood magic-bound with enchantment. He kept his eyes on her all evening, and when she left he ordered a servant to find out who this beautiful maiden was and where she lived.

The servant followed Cenerentola, but when she noticed this, she threw on the ground a handful of coins that she had got from the date tree. The servant stopped, lighted his lantern, and became so busy picking up all the coins that he quite forgot to follow her. Cenerentola was able to get home safely and change her clothes before the wicked sisters arrived.

The sisters, trying to make her envious, told her of all the fine things they had seen, but were quite unable to vex her.

The King was angry with his servant and warned him next time not to lose her.

Before long another ball was announced. Again the sisters went off to it, all bedecked in their finery, not at all concerned to leave poor Cenerentola at home on the kitchen hearth.

But Cenerentola, as soon as they disappeared, ran to the date tree and repeated the chant. Instantly there appeared a number of handmaidens: one with a looking glass, another with sweet-smelling rose water, others with curling irons and combs and pins, and rich apparel to dress her in. They groomed her so that she shone as gloriously as the sun, and they put her in a coach drawn by six white horses, attended by footmen and pages in handsome livery.

No sooner did Cenerentola appear in the ballroom than the

sisters were struck with amazement. And the King was quite overcome with love. His eyes never left her all evening.

When Cenerentola departed, the servant was again instructed to follow her. This time she was prepared with a handful of pearls. Seeing that these were not things to lose, the servant dropped behind to pick them up. And again she managed to slip away and remove her fine dress before her stepsisters saw her in it.

Meanwhile, the servant had returned slowly to the King, who cried out angrily when he saw him without the beautiful girl. "By the souls of my ancestors, if you do not find out who she is, you shall have such a thrashing as was never heard of before, and as many kicks as you have hairs in your beard!"

When the next ball was held, and the sisters were safely out of the house, Cenerentola went again to the date tree and once more repeated the chant. In an instant she found herself splendidly arrayed and seated in a coach of gold, with ever so many servants around her. She looked like a queen and made the sisters beside themselves with envy.

This time, when Cenerentola left the ballroom after the dancing, the King's servant kept close to the coach. She saw him running by the coach and cried to the coachman to drive on quickly. The coach set off at such a rattling pace that Cenerentola lost one of her beautiful slippers. The servant, being unable to keep up with the coach now, picked up the slipper and, carrying it to the King, told him all that had happened.

The King, turning the slipper around in his hand, said,

"You, indeed, are so beautiful it is no wonder that you belong to her. You who imprisoned her white foot are now binding my unhappy heart!"

The King then made a proclamation that all the women in the country should come to a banquet. For it, the most splendid provision was made – of pastas and pastries, of macaroni and sweetmeats – enough to feed an entire army. And when all the women were assembled, noble and lowly, rich and poor, beautiful and ugly, the King tried the slipper on each one. Thus he should see whom it fitted to a hair, and thus be able to discover the maiden he sought. But not one foot could fit the slipper.

When the King asked whether indeed every woman in the country was there, the Prince had to confess that he had one daughter at home. "But," said he, "Cenerentola sits always on the hearth, such a dirty, graceless girl that she is unworthy to come to your table."

But the King answered, "Let her be the very first, for so I order it."

All the guests departed, but the next day they assembled again, and with the ugly sisters came Cenerentola.

When the King saw Cenerentola, he began to wonder. But he said nothing.

After the feast came the trial of the slipper. This, as soon as ever it came near Cenerentola's foot, darted onto it as if of its own accord. The King ran to her, took her in his arms, and seated her under his royal canopy with a crown upon her head. And thereupon everyone bowed to her as their Queen.

Bastianelo

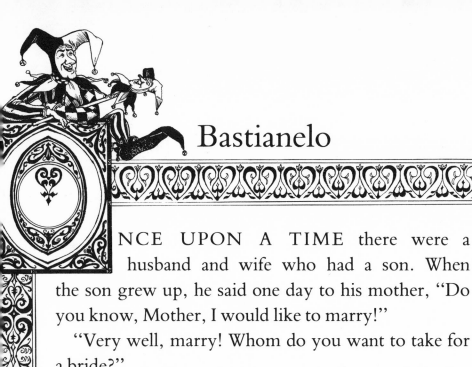

ONCE UPON A TIME there were a husband and wife who had a son. When the son grew up, he said one day to his mother, "Do you know, Mother, I would like to marry!"

"Very well, marry! Whom do you want to take for a bride?"

The son answered, "I want the gardener's daughter."

"She is a good girl; I am willing," said his mother.

He went and asked for the girl and her parents gave her to him, so they were married. All was merry, but in the midst of the wedding dinner the wine gave out. When the young husband cried, "There is no more wine!" the bride, to show that she was a good housekeeper, at once went to get some.

She carried the bottles to the cellar, turned the cock on the wine keg, and, waiting for the bottles to fill, began to think, "Suppose I should have a son, and we should call him Bastianelo, and he should die. Oh, how I should grieve! Oh, how I should grieve!" Thereupon she began to weep and wail, and the wine ran all over the cellar floor.

When the others saw that the bride did not return, her mother said, "I will go and see what the matter is." So she went into the cellar and saw the bride, with a bottle in her hand, weeping while the wine ran over the cellar. "What is it that makes you weep?"

"Ah! Mother, I was thinking that if I had a son and should name him Bastianelo, and he should die, oh, how I should grieve! Oh, how I should grieve!"

At this the mother, too, began to weep, and weep, and weep. And the wine ran all over the cellar.

When the people still at the table saw that no one was bringing the wine, the groom's father said, "I will go and see what is the matter. Certainly something has happened to the bride." He found the cellar full of wine, and the mother and bride weeping.

"What is the matter?" he asked. "Has anything wrong happened?"

"No," answered the bride, "but I was thinking that if I had a son and should call him Bastianelo, and he should die, oh, how I should grieve. Oh, how I should grieve!"

At this the father, too, began to weep. All three wept, and the wine ran all over the cellar.

When the groom saw that neither the bride nor the mother nor father came back, he decided, "Now I will go and see what the matter is." He went into the cellar and saw all the wine running over the cellar floor.

He hastened to stop the flow of wine, and then asked,

"What is the matter that you are all weeping, and have let the wine run all over the cellar?"

The bride admitted, "I was thinking that if I had a son and called him Bastianelo, and he should die, oh, how I should grieve! Oh, how I should grieve!"

The groom was astonished. "You stupid fools! Are you weeping at this and letting all the wine run into the cellar? Have you nothing else to think of? It shall never be said that I married such a one as you! I shall travel forth into the world, and until I find three fools greater than you, I shall not return here."

So the young man had a bread cake made for him, took a bottle of wine, a sausage, a change of clothing, and made up a bundle, which he tied on a stick and carried over his shoulder.

Day after day he journeyed and journeyed, but found no fools. At last, worn out, he was undecided whether to go on or to turn back. But then he said, "Oh, it is better to try a little longer."

So on he went, and shortly saw a man in his shirtsleeves at a well, all wet with perspiration and water. "What are you doing, sir, that you are so covered with water and in such a sweat?"

"Oh, let me alone!" the man answered. "I have been here a long time drawing water to fill this pail and I cannot fill it."

"What are you drawing the water in?" he asked the man.

"In this sieve."

"What are you thinking of, trying to draw water in a sieve? Just wait!" The young man went to a house nearby and borrowed a bucket. With this he returned to the well and filled the pail.

"Thank you, good man. God knows how long I should have had to remain here!"

"Here is one," said the young man, "who is a greater fool than my wife."

He continued on his journey and after a time saw at a distance a man in his shirt who was jumping from a tree. He drew near and saw a woman under the same tree holding a pair of breeches. When he asked them what they were doing, they said they had been there a long time. The man was trying on the breeches and did not know how to get into them. "I have jumped and jumped," said the man, "until I am tired out, and I still cannot imagine how to get into those breeches."

"Well," said the traveler, "you might stay here forever. You would never get into them this way. Come down, now, and lean against the tree."

He took the man's legs then and put them into the breeches. After he had done this, he asked, "Is that right?"

"Very good, bless you," said the man. "If it had not been for you, God knows how long I should have had to continue jumping."

Now the traveler said to himself, "I have seen two fools greater than my wife." And he went on his way.

As he approached a city he heard a great noise. When he drew near, he asked what it was all about and learned that there was a wedding. It was the custom in that city for brides to enter the city gate on horseback. This time there was going on a great discussion between the groom and the owner of the horse, for the bride was tall and the horse was high. They could not get through the gate; either they must cut off the bride's head or chop off the horse's legs. The groom naturally did not wish his bride's head cut off, and the owner of the horse refused to have his horse lose his legs. Hence the uproar.

The traveler said, "Wait." He turned to the bride and slapped the top of her head so that she lowered it. At the same time he kicked the horse. They passed through the gate into the city.

In return for this help, the groom and the owner of the horse asked the young man what present they could give him. He answered that he did not wish for anything, and to himself counted, "Two and one make three! That is enough! Now I will go home."

This he did, and said to his wife, "Here I am, my wife; I have seen three greater fools than you. Let us remain in peace and think of nothing else."

Now they went on with the wedding celebration, and always after that they lived in peace.

After a time the wife bore a son whom they named Bastianelo – but Bastianelo did not die. He still lives with his father and mother.

Japan

The Tongue-cut Sparrow

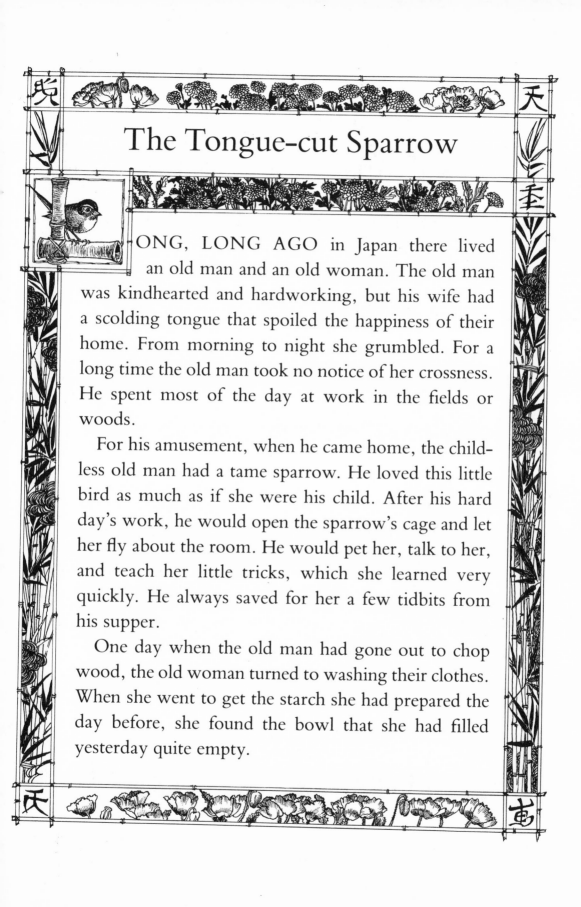

LONG, LONG AGO in Japan there lived an old man and an old woman. The old man was kindhearted and hardworking, but his wife had a scolding tongue that spoiled the happiness of their home. From morning to night she grumbled. For a long time the old man took no notice of her crossness. He spent most of the day at work in the fields or woods.

For his amusement, when he came home, the childless old man had a tame sparrow. He loved this little bird as much as if she were his child. After his hard day's work, he would open the sparrow's cage and let her fly about the room. He would pet her, talk to her, and teach her little tricks, which she learned very quickly. He always saved for her a few tidbits from his supper.

One day when the old man had gone out to chop wood, the old woman turned to washing their clothes. When she went to get the starch she had prepared the day before, she found the bowl that she had filled yesterday quite empty.

While she stood wondering who could have taken the starch, down flew the pet sparrow. Bowing her feathered head – a trick she had been taught by her master – the honest little bird confessed:

"It is I who have taken the starch. I thought it was food put out for me, and I ate it all. I beg you to forgive me."

But the old woman was not willing to forgive. She had never loved the sparrow and indeed had often complained to her husband about the extra work she created. Now she was only too happy to find a reason to scold the pet. But she was not content with using harsh words. In a fit of rage, she seized the sparrow and cut off her tongue.

"You took my starch with that tongue! Now you shall see what it is like to go without it." With these words she drove the bird away, without the slightest pity for its suffering.

The old woman then prepared more rice starch, grumbling as she did so, and spread the starched clothes on boards to dry in the sun.

In the evening the old man came home, looking forward as usual to seeing his pet. But tonight the old man was to be disappointed.

Hastily he drew off his straw sandals and stepped onto the veranda. No sparrow was to be seen. He called his wife and asked anxiously:

"Where is Suzume San [Miss Sparrow] today?"

At first, the old woman pretended not to know.

"Your sparrow? I am sure I don't know. Come to think

of it, I haven't seen her all afternoon. I shouldn't wonder if the ungrateful bird had flown away and left you."

But at last, when the old man gave her no peace and had asked her again and again, she confessed. She told him crossly how the sparrow had eaten the rice paste she had made for starching her clothes, and how when the sparrow had confessed to what she had done, she had taken her scissors and cut off the sparrow's tongue. Finally, she had driven the bird away.

"How could you be so cruel? Oh! how could you be so cruel?" said the old man over and over.

"Poor Suzume San! She won't be able to sing anymore. And the pain of the cutting must have made her ill. Is there nothing to be done?"

After his cross old wife had gone to sleep, the old man shed many tears. Then a bright thought comforted him. Tomorrow he would go look for the sparrow. At last he was able to fall asleep.

The next morning he rose early, as soon as ever the day broke, and snatching a hasty breakfast, started out over the hills and through the woods. At every clump of bamboos he stopped to cry:

"Where, oh where, does my tongue-cut sparrow stay? Where, oh where, does my tongue-cut sparrow stay?"

He did not stop to rest for a noonday meal, but kept on far into the afternoon until he found himself near a large bamboo wood. There, sure enough, at the edge of the wood, he saw his own dear sparrow waiting to welcome him. He ran forward

joyfully to greet her. She bowed her little head and went through a number of the tricks her master had taught her, to show her pleasure at seeing her old friend again. And, wonderful to relate, she could talk as of old. The old man told her of his grief, but the sparrow begged him to think no more about the past, for she was quite well now.

In his joy the old man forgot how tired he was. His lost sparrow was found and she was well. He knew that she was no common bird; he would call her now the Lady Sparrow.

The Lady Sparrow asked the old man to follow her. Flying ahead, she led him to a beautiful house in the heart of the bamboo grove. The old man entered it in astonishment. It was built of the whitest wood. Its soft cream-colored mats were the finest he had ever seen, and the cushions that the sparrow brought out for him to sit on were made of the richest silk. Rare vases and lacquered boxes adorned the *tokonoma*, the alcove for precious objects, in every room.

The Lady Sparrow led the old man to the place of honor. Then, resting at a humble distance, she thanked him with polite bows for the kindness he had shown her so many long years. She introduced her family, and her lovely daughters brought in a feast so delicious that the old man thought he must be dreaming. In the middle of the dinner some of the daughters amused their guest by performing the *Suzume-odori*, the "Sparrow's dance."

Never had the old man enjoyed himself so much. The hours flew by too quickly. The darkness of nighttime reminded him that his journey home was a long one and he must take his leave. He thanked his hostess for her splendid entertainment and begged her to forget all she had suffered. Now that he knew all was well with her, he could return home with a light heart. If ever she wanted him for anything, she had only to send for him and he would come at once.

The Lady Sparrow begged him to stay and rest, but the old man said he must return to his old wife, who would be cross because he had not come home at the usual time. Now that he knew where the Lady Sparrow lived, he would come to see her whenever he could spare the time.

Since the Lady Sparrow could not persuade him to stay longer, she gave an order to some of her servants and at once they brought two wicker baskets—one heavy and the other light. These were placed before the old man, and the Lady Sparrow asked him to choose one of them for a present. The old man could not refuse and chose the lighter basket, saying:

"I am now too old to carry the heavy basket."

The sparrows all helped to hoist the basket onto the old man's back and went to the gate to see him off, bidding him good-bye with many bows and entreating him to come again whenever he could.

At home, just as he expected, the old man found his wife even crosser than usual. It was late and she had been waiting up for him.

"Where have you been all this time?" she shouted.

The old man tried to pacify her with the basket of presents. He told her of all that had happened, and how wonderfully he had been entertained at the sparrow's house.

"Let us see what is in the basket," said the old man, not giving her time to grumble again. "You must help me open it."

To their utter astonishment, they found the basket filled with gold and silver coins and precious jewels. The mats of their little cottage fairly glittered as they laid out the gifts and handled them over and over again. The old man was overjoyed. The riches would enable him to give up his hard work and live in ease the rest of his days.

"Thanks to my good little sparrow. Thanks to my good little sparrow," he repeated many times.

But the old woman, after her first surprise and satisfaction at the sight of the gold and silver, could not suppress the greed of her wicked nature. She began to reproach the old man for not having brought home the heavy basket of presents. In his innocence he had told her how he had refused the heavier one.

"You silly old man," she screamed. "Why did you not bring

home the heavy basket. Think of what we have lost! We might have had twice as much silver and gold as this. You are certainly an old fool."

The old man wished that he had said nothing about the heavier one, but it was too late. The old woman, not content with the good luck that had so unexpectedly befallen them and that she so little deserved, made up her mind to get more if possible.

Early the next morning, she made the old man describe the way to the sparrow's house. When he saw what was in her mind, he tried to keep her from going, but it was useless. Her greed made her forget her cruel treatment of the sparrow.

Ever since the Lady Sparrow had returned home in her sad plight, her family had talked about the old woman's wickedness. "How could she inflict so heavy a punishment for such an innocent offense?" They all loved the kind and patient old man, but they hated the old woman. If ever they had the chance, they would punish her as she deserved.

They had not long to wait.

After walking for several hours, the old woman at last found the bamboo grove that her husband had described. She stood before it and cried:

"Where is the tongue-cut sparrow's house? Where is the tongue-cut sparrow's house?"

At last she noticed the eaves of the house sticking out from the bamboo foliage. She hastened to the door and knocked loudly.

When the servants told the Lady Sparrow that her old mistress

was at the door asking to see her, she was indeed surprised. She wondered not a little at the boldness of the old woman in coming to the house. But the Lady Sparrow was polite. She went out to greet the visitor.

The old woman wasted no time. Without shame, she went right to the point.

"You need not trouble to entertain me as you did my old man. I have come to get the basket that he so stupidly left behind. I shall soon take my leave if you will give me the heavy basket. That is all I want."

The Lady Sparrow at once ordered her servants to bring out the heavy basket, which the old woman eagerly seized. She hoisted it onto her back and, without stopping to thank the Lady Sparrow, hurried homewards.

The basket was so heavy that she could not walk fast. Often she had to sit down and rest. While she staggered along, her desire to open the basket grew greater and greater. Finally, the greedy old woman could wait no longer. She set the basket

down by the wayside and opened it carefully, expecting to gloat over gold and silver and jewels.

What the old woman saw so terrified her that she nearly lost her senses. Horrible demons bounded out of the basket and surrounded her as if they intended to kill her. Not even in nightmares had she seen such frightful-looking creatures. A demon with one huge eye in the middle of its forehead glared at her; monsters with wide, gaping mouths opened them further as if to devour her; a huge snake began to coil and hiss; and a giant frog hopped toward her, croaking.

Never had the old woman been so frightened. She ran from the spot as fast as her quaking legs would carry her. At home she fell to the floor in tears, and told her husband all that had happened to her.

She began to blame the sparrow, but the old man stopped her at once. "Don't blame the sparrow. It is your wickedness that has at last met its reward. I only hope this may be a lesson to you in the future."

The old woman said nothing more. From that day she repented. By degrees she became such a good old woman that her husband hardly knew her to be the same person. They lived their last days together happily, free from want or care, spending carefully the treasure the old man had received from his beloved pet, the tongue-cut sparrow.

The White Hare and the Crocodiles

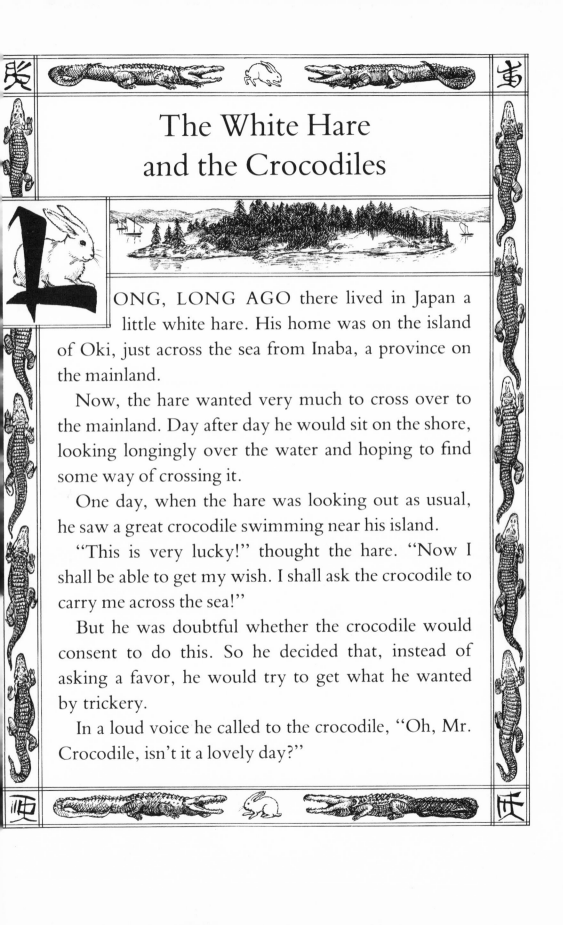

LONG, LONG AGO there lived in Japan a little white hare. His home was on the island of Oki, just across the sea from Inaba, a province on the mainland.

Now, the hare wanted very much to cross over to the mainland. Day after day he would sit on the shore, looking longingly over the water and hoping to find some way of crossing it.

One day, when the hare was looking out as usual, he saw a great crocodile swimming near his island.

"This is very lucky!" thought the hare. "Now I shall be able to get my wish. I shall ask the crocodile to carry me across the sea!"

But he was doubtful whether the crocodile would consent to do this. So he decided that, instead of asking a favor, he would try to get what he wanted by trickery.

In a loud voice he called to the crocodile, "Oh, Mr. Crocodile, isn't it a lovely day?"

The crocodile swam nearer the shore, very pleased to hear a voice. He had come out all by himself that day to enjoy the bright sunshine, was just beginning to feel a bit lonely, when the hare's cheerful greeting broke the silence.

"I wonder who it was that spoke to me just now. Was it you, Mr. Hare? You must be lonely all by yourself."

"Oh, no, I am not at all lonely," said the hare. "It is such a fine day I just came out on the beach to enjoy myself. Won't you stop awhile and play with me?"

The crocodile pulled himself out of the sea and the two played games together for some time. Then the hare said:

"Mr. Crocodile, you live in the sea and I live on this island, and we do not often meet, so I know very little about you. Tell me, do you think the number of crocodiles is greater than the number of hares?"

"Of course, there are more crocodiles than hares," answered the crocodile. "Can you not see that for yourself? You live on this small island, while I live in the sea, which spreads through all parts of the world. If I should call together all the crocodiles who dwell in the sea, you hares would be as nothing compared to us!" The crocodile sounded very conceited.

The hare, who meant to play a trick on the crocodile, answered:

"Do you think it possible for you to call up enough crocodiles to form a line from this island across the sea to Inaba?"

The crocodile thought for a moment.

"Of course, it is possible."

"Then do try," said the artful hare, "and I will count the number from here."

The crocodile, who was simpleminded and hadn't the least idea that the hare intended to play a trick on him, agreed to do what the hare asked.

"Wait a moment, while I go back into the sea and call my company together."

The crocodile plunged into the sea and was gone for some time. The hare, meanwhile, waited patiently on the shore. At last the crocodile appeared, bringing with him a large number of other crocodiles.

"Look, Mr. Hare!" said the crocodile. "It is nothing for my friends to form a line between here and Inaba. There are enough crocodiles to stretch even as far as China or India. Did you ever see so many crocodiles?"

The whole company of crocodiles then arranged themselves in the water so as to form a bridge between the island of Oki and the mainland of Inaba. When the hare saw the bridge of crocodiles, he said:

"How splendid! I did not believe this was possible. Now let me count you all. To do this, however, with your permission I must walk on your backs over to the other side, so please be so good as not to move, or else I shall fall into the sea and be drowned."

The hare hopped off the island onto the strange bridge of crocodiles, counting as he jumped from one crocodile's back to the other:

"Please keep quite still, or I shall not be able to count. One, two, three, four, five, six, seven, eight, nine . . ."

Thus the cunning hare walked right across to the mainland of Inaba. Not content with getting his wish, he now began to jeer at the crocodiles instead of thanking them. As he leaped off the last one's back, he said, "Oh, you stupid crocodiles, now I have done with you!"

He aimed to run away as fast as he could, but he did not escape so easily. As soon as the crocodiles understood that the hare had played a trick on them to enable him to cross the sea, and that he was now laughing at them for their stupidity, they became angry and determined to take revenge. They ran after the hare and caught him. Then they surrounded the poor little animal and pulled out all his fur. He begged them to spare him and cried out loudly, but with each tuft of his fur they pulled out, the crocodiles said:

"This serves you right."

When the crocodiles had pulled out the last bit of fur, they threw the poor hare onto the beach and swam away, laughing at what they had done.

The hare was now a pitiful sight. His beautiful white fur

was gone, and his bare little body quivered with pain. He lay on the beach and wept for his misfortune. Although his suffering was due to his own trickery, no one could help feeling sorry for him. The crocodiles had been cruel indeed.

At this moment, a number of youths arrayed like a king's sons happened to pass by. Seeing the hare lying there on the beach crying, they asked him what the matter was.

The hare lifted up his head from between his paws and said:

"I had a fight with some crocodiles, but I was beaten. They pulled out all my fur and left me here to suffer—that is why I am crying."

One of the young men pretended kindness, and said to the hare:

"I feel sorry for you, and I know of a remedy that will cure your sore body. You must bathe in the sea, and then sit in the wind. This will make your fur grow again, and you will be just as you were before."

The young men went on, leaving the hare very pleased to think he had found a cure. At once he bathed in the sea and then sat where the wind could blow upon him.

But as the breezes blew and dried him, the hare's skin became tight and it stiffened. And the salt from the seawater increased the pain so greatly that he rolled on the sand in agony and cried aloud.

Just then another young man passed by, carrying a great bag on his back. He saw the hare, and asked why he was crying so loudly.

The poor hare, remembering how he had been deceived by

one very like the man who now spoke to him, did not answer, but continued to cry.

This man, however, had a kind heart. He looked at the hare pityingly and said:

"You poor thing. I see that your fur has been all pulled out and your skin is quite bare. Who can have treated you so cruelly?"

When the hare heard these kind words, he was encouraged and told the man all that had befallen him. The little animal hid nothing from his friend, but confessed how he had played a trick on the crocodiles and had jeered at them for their stupidity. Then he told how the crocodiles had revenged themselves on him, and how he had been fooled by a party of young men who looked very like his new kind friend. The hare ended his tale of woe by begging the man to give him medicine that would make his fur grow again.

The man looked down at the hare.

"I am very sorry for all you have suffered, but you must remember that it was only the result of your deceit."

"I know," answered the sorrowful hare, "but I have repented and made up my mind never to be deceitful again. I beg you to tell me how I may cure my sore body and make my fur grow again."

"I will help you," said the man. "First, you must bathe well in that pond of fresh water over there, and wash away all the salt. Next you must pick some of those *gama* spikes★ growing

★ Cat-o'-nine-tails or bulrushes.

near the edge of the water, spread them on the ground, and roll yourself on them. If you will do this, your fur will grow again, and you will be quite well again in only a little while."

The hare was delighted to be told in such a kindly way exactly what he must do. He crawled over to the pond and bathed himself carefully. He picked the *gama* spikes and rolled himself over the blossoms.

To his amazement, even as he was doing this, the hare saw fine white fur begin to grow again on his body. His pain soon ceased and he felt just as usual.

Hopping joyfully over to his benefactor and kneeling at his feet, the hare looked up.

"I cannot express my thanks well enough for all you have done for me. It is my earnest wish to do something for you in return. Please tell me who you are."

"I am no king's son as you think but a great-great-great-grandson of the younger brother of the Sun Goddess. My name is Okuni-nushi-no-Mikoto," answered the man. "Those beings who passed here before me are my half-brothers. They have heard of a beautiful princess called Yakami who lives in this province of Inaba, and they are on their way to find her and to ask her to marry one of them. On this journey I am only an attendant, so I walk behind them with this great bag on my back."

Humbling himself before this great being, the hare replied:

"It is impossible to believe that that unkind fellow who sent me to bathe in the sea is one of your brothers. I am quite sure that the Princess will refuse to become the bride of any one of them. She will prefer you for your goodness of heart."

Okuni now bid the little animal good-bye and, going quickly on his way, soon overtook his brothers—just as they were entering the Princess's gate.

Exactly as the hare had predicted, the Princess would not be persuaded to become the bride of any of the brothers. But when she looked at the kind young man who was a great-great-great-grandson of the younger brother of the Sun Goddess, she went straight up to him and said:

"It is to you I give myself."

Thus it came about that Okuni and the Princess called Yakami were married. The hare became famous as "The White Hare of Inaba," but what became of the crocodiles nobody knows.

Norway

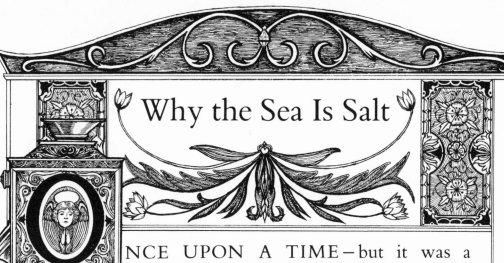

Why the Sea Is Salt

ONCE UPON A TIME—but it was a long, long time ago—there were two brothers. One of them was rich and one was poor.

On a Christmas Eve, the poor one had not so much as a crumb in the house, either of meat or of bread. So he went to his brother to ask him for something with which to keep Christmas. It was not the first time he had called upon his rich brother for help, and since the rich one was stingy, the poor brother was not made very welcome.

The rich brother said, "If you will go away and never come back, I'll give you a whole side of bacon."

The poor brother, full of thanks, agreed to this.

"Well, here is the bacon," said the rich brother. "Now go straight away to the Land of Hunger."

The poor brother took the bacon and set off. He walked the whole day, and at dusk he came to a place where he saw a very bright light.

"Maybe this is the place," said he and turned aside. The first person he saw was an old, old man, with a long white beard, who was chopping wood for the Christmas fire.

"Good even," said the man with the bacon.

"The same to you. Where are you going so late in the day?" asked the man.

"Oh, I'm going to the Land of Hunger, if only I can find the right way."

"Well, you are not far wrong, for this is that land," said the old man. "When you go inside, everyone there will want to buy your bacon, for meat is scarce here. But mind you don't sell it unless you get for it the hand mill, which stands behind the door. When you come out again, I'll teach you how to handle the mill. You will be able to make it grind almost anything."

The man with the bacon thanked the other for his good advice. Then he gave a great knock at the door.

When he had entered, everything happened just as the old man had said it would. Everyone came swarming up to him like ants around an anthill. Each one tried to outbid the other for the bacon.

"Well," said the man, "by rights it is my wife and I who should have this bacon for Christmas dinner. However, since you have all set your hearts on it, I suppose I must let you have it. But if I do sell it, I must have in exchange that mill behind the door."

At first they wouldn't hear of such a bargain. They chaffered and they haggled with the man. But he stuck to his bargain, and at last they had to part with the mill.

The man now carried the mill out into the yard and asked the old woodcutter how to handle it. As soon as the old man had shown him how to make it grind, he thanked him and hurried off home as fast as he could. But the clock had struck twelve on this Christmas Eve before he reached his own door.

"Wherever in the world have you been?" complained his wife. "Here I have sat hour after hour waiting and watching, without so much as two sticks to lay together under the Christmas broth."

"Well," said the man, "I couldn't get back before because I had to go a long way—first for one thing, and then for another. But now you shall see what you shall see!"

Carefully he set the mill on the table. First of all, he ordered it to grind lights. Next he asked for a tablecloth, then for meat, then ale, and so on till he and his wife had every kind of thing to help them celebrate Christmas. He had only to speak the word, and the mill would grind out anything he asked for. His wife stood by blessing her stars. She kept on asking where he had got this wonderful mill, but he wouldn't tell her.

"It's all one where I got it. You can see the mill is a good one. That's enough."

The man ground meat and drink and sweets enough to last till Twelfth Day. On the Third Day, he asked all his friends and kin to his house and gave a great feast.

When the rich brother arrived and saw all that was on the

table, and all that was stored behind in the larder, he grew spiteful and wild. He couldn't bear it that his brother should have anything. It made him shout: "It was only on Christmas Eve that my brother was so poor he came and begged for a morsel of food! Now he gives a feast as if he were a count or a king!"

The rich man demanded of his brother, "How did you get all this wealth?"

"From behind the door," answered the new owner of the mill. He did not intend to give away his secret. But later on in the evening, when he was quite merry, he could keep his secret no longer. He brought out the mill and said, "There, you see what has given me all this wealth." And he made the mill grind all kinds of things.

When the rich brother beheld this, his heart was set on having the mill. And he got it, after much coaxing. But he had to pay three hundred dollars for it, and leave it with his brother until hay harvest. His brother thought that, if he kept it until then, he could make it grind meat and drink to last for years.

You may know that the mill did not grow rusty for lack of work to do.

When hay harvest came around, the rich brother got the mill, but the other took care not to teach him how to handle it.

It was evening when the rich brother took the mill home. Next morning, he told his wife to go out into the field and toss hay. He would stay at home and get the dinner ready.

When dinnertime drew near, he put the mill on the kitchen

table and ordered, "Grind herrings and broth, and grind them good and fast."

The mill began at once to grind the herrings and broth. First, they filled every dish in the house, then all the big tubs, and then they flowed all over the kitchen floor.

Madly, the man twisted and twirled at the mill to get it to stop. But for all his twisting and fingering, the mill went on grinding.

In a little while, the broth rose so high that the man was about to drown. He managed to throw open the kitchen door and run into the parlor. But it wasn't long before the mill had ground the parlor full, too. It was at the risk of his life that the man reached the doorlatch through the stream of broth.

When he had managed to pull the door open, he ran out and off down the road. A stream of herrings and broth poured out at his heels, roaring like a waterfall over the whole farm.

His wife, who was still in the field tossing hay, began to think it a long time to dinner. At last she said:

"Well, even though the master hasn't called us home, we may as well go. Maybe he finds it hard work to boil the broth, and will be glad of my help."

The men were willing enough to go. But just as they had climbed a little way up the hill, what should they meet but herrings and broth, all running and dashing and splashing together in a stream. The master himself was running ahead for his very life.

As he passed the workers, he bawled out:

"If only each of you could drink with a hundred throats! Take care you are not drowned in the broth."

Away he went, as fast as he could, to his brother's house. He begged him to take back the mill at once.

"If it grinds only one hour more, the whole parish will be swallowed up by herrings and broth."

But his brother wouldn't hear of taking it back until the other paid him three hundred dollars more.

So now the poor brother had both the money and the mill.

It wasn't long before he set up a farmhouse far finer than the one in which his brother lived. With the mill, he ground so much gold that he covered the house with it.

Since the farm lay by the seaside, the golden house gleamed and glistened far away to ships at sea. All who sailed by put to shore to see the rich man in his golden house, and to see the wonderful mill. Its fame spread far and wide, till there was nobody who hadn't heard tell of it.

One day a skipper sailed in to see the mill. The first thing he asked was whether it could grind salt.

"Grind salt!" said the owner. "I should think it could. It can grind anything."

When the skipper heard that, he said he must have the mill, cost what it would. If only he had it, he thought he would no longer have to take long voyages across stormy seas for a cargo of salt.

At first the man wouldn't hear of parting with his mill. But the skipper begged so hard that at last he let him have it. However, the skipper had to pay a great deal of money for it.

When the skipper had the mill on his back, he went off with it at once. He was afraid the man would change his mind, so he took no time to ask how to handle the mill. He got on board his ship as fast as he could, and set sail.

When the skipper had sailed a good way off, he brought the mill up on deck and said:

"Grind salt, and grind both good and fast."

Well, the mill began to grind salt so that it poured out like water.

When the skipper had filled the ship, he wished to stop the mill. But whichever way he turned it, and however much he tried, it was no good. The mill kept grinding on, and the heap of salt grew higher and higher. At last it sank the ship.

Now the mill lies at the bottom of the sea. It grinds away at this very day, and that is why the sea is salt.

The Three Billy Goats Gruff

ONCE UPON A TIME there were three billy goats, who were to go up to the hillside to make themselves fat. The name of all three was Gruff.

On the way up, they had to cross a bridge over a stream. Under the bridge lived a great ugly troll, with eyes as big as saucers, and a nose as long as a poker.

First of all over the bridge came the youngest billy goat Gruff.

Trip, trap! Trip, trap! went the bridge.

"WHO'S THAT TRIPPING OVER MY BRIDGE?" roared the troll.

"Oh, it is only I, the tiniest billy goat Gruff. I'm going up to the hillside to make myself fat," said the billy goat – with such a small voice!

"NOW I'M COMING TO GOBBLE YOU UP," said the troll.

"Oh, no, pray don't take *me*. I'm too little, that I am," said the billy goat. "Wait a bit till the second billy goat Gruff comes; he's much bigger."

"WELL, BE OFF WITH YOU," said the troll.

A little later, up came the second billy goat Gruff to cross the bridge.

Trip, trap! Trip, trap! Trip, trap! went the bridge.

"WHO'S THAT TRIPPING OVER MY BRIDGE?" roared the troll.

"Oh, it's the second billy goat Gruff, and I'm going up to the hillside to make myself fat," said the billy goat. His voice was not so small, either.

"NOW I'M COMING TO GOBBLE YOU UP," said the troll.

"Oh, no, don't take *me.* Wait a little till the big billy goat Gruff comes. He's much bigger."

Just then, up came the big billy goat Gruff.

Trip, trap! Trip, trap! Trip, trap! Trip, trap! went the bridge.

This billy goat was so heavy that the bridge creaked and groaned under him.

"WHO'S THAT TRIPPING OVER MY BRIDGE?" roared the troll.

"IT'S I! THE BIG BILLY GOAT GRUFF," said the billy goat. He had an ugly hoarse voice of his own.

"NOW I'M COMING TO GOBBLE YOU UP," roared the troll.

"WELL, COME ALONG!
I'VE GOT TWO SPEARS,
AND I'LL POKE YOUR EYEBALLS
OUT AT YOUR EARS:
I'VE GOT BESIDES
TWO GREAT BIG STONES

AND I'LL CRUSH YOU TO BITS,
BODY AND BONES."

That was what the big billy goat said. He flew at the troll and poked his eyes out with his horns. He crushed him to bits, body and bones, and tossed him out into the stream. Then he went up to the hillside. There the billy goats got so fat they were scarcely able to walk home again. If the fat hasn't fallen off them, why, they're still fat; and so . . .

Snip, snap, snout,
This tale's told out.

Poland

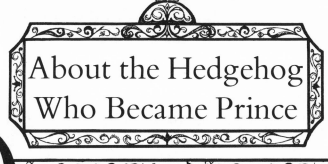

About the Hedgehog Who Became Prince

ONCE UPON A TIME in Poland, there lived a man and his wife who were jolly enough, and contented, except for one thing. No baby lay kicking in the cradle that hung from a hook in the ceiling.

The man hadn't much time to worry about this; he was busy all day in the fields. But his wife sometimes fretted about it.

One day the wife was gathering berries in the woods. Suddenly she saw a hedgehog lying under a fern. With a loud sigh she said, "Oh, if I had even a hedgehog for a baby, I would praise God."

Now, the good woman did not know that Jendza the Witch was sitting in a bush near her and had heard what she said.

Soon after this, the woman had her wish. A baby was born. But instead of having blue eyes, downy hair, and hands and feet like a human baby, this one was covered all over with sharp, prickly quills. In short, it was neither more nor less than a baby hedgehog.

"Well, I'm blessed!" said the woman. "Who would have thought that my words would come true like this! I said, 'Even if I had a hedgehog for a baby, I would praise God'—and here it is."

"Well, it is better than nothing," replied her husband. "Let us be thankful for what has come to us."

The man and his wife took good care of the little hedgehog and became fond of it. It never grew very much, and it never talked. Always it sat in the cradle.

Then one day when the woman was busy washing and felt tired, it spoke and said: "Mother, I'll take Father's dinner to him today."

And from that day everybody was surprised to see the hedgehog carrying its father's dinner to him!

A few years later it said: "Mother, I'll take the pigs to feed in the wood."

And for the next six years this was its work. As it watched the pigs, it sat under a mushroom, and never was even a single pig missing.

One day the King came riding through the wood. He had lost his way. He hunted and hunted for the path, but could not find it.

"What is Your Majesty looking for?" asked the hedgehog. The King looked around and up and down, wondering where the voice came from. At last he saw the hedgehog under the mushroom.

"I have lost my way," he replied.

"I will show it to you," said the hedgehog. "But first you must promise to give me one of your daughters in marriage."

"By all means," said the King with a polite smile. He thought to himself as he said it: "It will do no harm to make this promise. Nothing will come of it."

"Your Majesty's word is not enough," said the hedgehog. "You must write it down and give me your handkerchief as a pledge."

The King was not pleased at this. He did not want a hedgehog for a son-in-law. But then he did not want to spend the night in the cold forest and be eaten by wolves, so he was obliged to write it down.

He gave the paper and the handkerchief to the hedgehog, who then guided him out of the wood. He rode back to his palace and the hedgehog took the pigs home.

A few years later, the hedgehog said: "Father, please have a saddle made for the cock, for I must ride out into the world."

A saddle was made for the cock and the hedgehog got on its back.

"Where are you going?" asked the mother.

"Don't ask me that, Mother," replied the hedgehog, and off he set on his ride into the world.

Over valley and mountain, over meadow and hill the hedgehog rode on the cock's back until they came to the palace of the King.

"What do you want?" asked the guardsman at the gate.

"I want to see the King," replied the hedgehog.

"Impossible!" said the guardsman. "The King is at dinner." But when the hedgehog showed him the King's handkerchief, he was obliged to open the gate.

What a shock for the King to have the cock come flying in with the hedgehog on its back! The King was vexed, but a King's written word must be kept; so he asked his three daughters which one would consent to marry the hedgehog.

At the very idea, the Princesses nearly split their sides with laughing. "Who ever heard of a Princess marrying a hedgehog?" they cried.

The King flew into a rage at the hedgehog. "I'll have you killed!" he cried, and he ordered his guardsman to shoot the hedgehog.

At once the hedgehog gave a shrill whistle.

From every side, from near and far, hedgehogs came crawling. They came in at the windows and at the doors. They climbed up on the tables and up on the chairs. And as each one crawled by, it stuck its quills into the people near it.

Now, of course, these were not hedgehogs at all, but good fairies.

The King and Princesses, and all the Court, were hopping about with the pricks of the quills. They rubbed their legs and howled with pain.

"Stop, stop, stop!" cried the King. "You *shall* have one of my daughters!" And he commanded his youngest to marry the hedgehog.

The Princess dressed in finery and the hedgehog got on the cock's back. Thus they went to the church.

When the marriage ceremony was over, the bride turned to walk out with the bridegroom. Wonder of wonders! Instead of the hedgehog, there stood a handsome young man, who made a low bow to the bride and offered his arm in a princely manner.

"Thank you, Princess," he said. "You have broken the spell that Jendza the Witch cast over me at my birth."

The Princess was delighted with her princely young man,

and the King with his new son-in-law. The young man told them about his good parents, and they were sent for, to live near the palace. The King made his son-in-law heir to his throne.

And that night a grand ball and feast were given such as had never been enjoyed before or since.

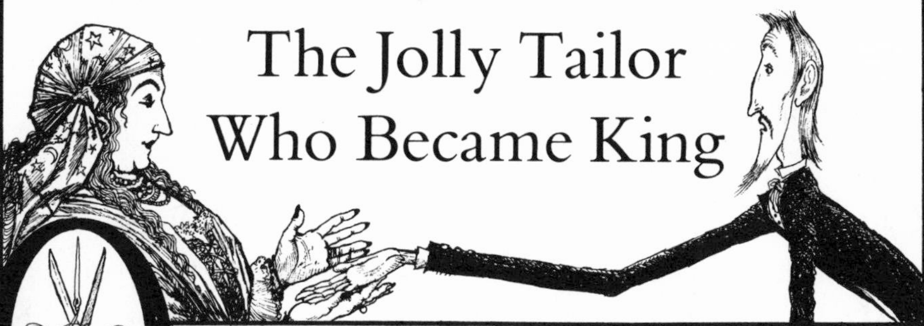

The Jolly Tailor Who Became King

ONCE UPON A TIME, in the town of Taidaraida, there lived a merry little tailor, Mr. Joseph Nitechka. He was a very thin man and had a small beard of one hundred and thirty-six hairs.

All tailors are thin, reminding one of a needle and thread, but Mr. Nitechka was the thinnest of all. He could pass through the eye of his own needle. He was so thin that he could eat nothing but noodles, for they were the only things that could go down his throat. But for all this, he was a very happy man, and a handsome one, too, particularly on holidays, when he braided his beard.

Now, Mr. Nitechka would have lived very happily in Taidaraida had it not been for a gypsy. She happened to be in the town when she cut her foot. In her trouble she went to the tailor, who darned the skin so carefully and so neatly that not a scar could be seen. The gypsy was so grateful that she read Nitechka's future from his hand:

"If you leave this town on a Sunday and walk always westward, you will reach a place where you will be chosen King."

Nitechka laughed at this. But that very night he dreamed that he indeed became a King, and that from great prosperity he grew so fat that he looked like an immense barrel. Upon waking he thought:

"Maybe it is true – who knows? Get up, Mr. Nitechka, and go west."

He took a bundle with a hundred needles and a thousand miles of thread, a thimble, an iron, and a pair of very big scissors, and started out to find the West. He asked first one and then another in the town of Taidaraida where the West was. But no one knew. Finally he asked an old man, a hundred and six years old, who after thinking awhile said:

"West must be there, where the sun sets."

This seemed so wise to Nitechka that he went that way. But he had not gone far when a gust of wind blew across the field – not a very strong gust, but, because Mr. Nitechka was so exceedingly thin, just strong enough to carry him off.

The tailor flew through the air, laughing heartily at such a ride. Soon, however, the wind became tired and let him down to earth. He was much bewildered and did not come to his senses until someone shouted:

"What is this?"

Mr. Nitechka looked around and saw that he was in a wheat field and that the wind had thrown him right into the arms of a scarecrow. The scarecrow was very elegant in a blue jacket and a broken stovepipe hat, and his trousers were only a little bit torn. He had two sticks for feet and also sticks for hands.

Nitechka took off his little cap, bowed very low, and said in his thin voice:

"My regards to the honorable sir. I beg your pardon if I stepped on your foot. I am Mr. Nitechka, the tailor."

"I am pleased to meet such a charming man," answered the scarecrow. "I am Count Scarecrow, and my coat of arms is four sticks. I watch the sparrows here so that they will not steal wheat, but I give little heed to them. I am uncommonly courageous and would like to fight only with lions and tigers. This year, however, they very seldom come to eat the wheat. Where are you going, Mr. Nitechka?"

Nitechka bowed again and hopped three times, as he was very polite and knew that well-bred men greeted each other thus.

"Where do I go, Mr. Count? I am going westward to a place where I shall become King."

"Is it possible?"

"Of course! I was born to be a King. And perhaps you, Mr. Count, would like to go with me. It will be merrier."

"All right," answered the scarecrow. "I am already weary of being here. But please, Mr. Nitechka, mend my clothes a bit. I might like to marry someone on the way, and so I should be neat and handsome."

"With great pleasure!" said Nitechka. He went to work,

and in an hour the scarecrow had a beautiful suit and a hat almost like new. The sparrows in the field laughed at him a little, but he paid no attention to them as he walked with great dignity beside Mr. Nitechka.

On the way the two became great friends. They generally slept in a wheat field, the tailor tying himself to the scarecrow with a piece of thread so that the wind could not carry him off again. And when dogs fell upon them, the scarecrow, who was very brave because of his profession, tore out his foot and threw it after them. Then he tied it again to his body.

They continued on their way toward Pacanów, a beautiful old town, where the King had died. After seven days of adventure they reached it.

They were greatly astonished to see that all around Pacanów it was sunshiny and pleasant. But directly over Pacanów, the rain poured from the sky as from a bucket.

"I won't go in there," said the scarecrow, "because my hat will get wet."

"And even I do not wish to become King of such a wet kingdom," said the tailor.

Just then the townspeople spied them and rushed toward them, led by the burgomaster riding on a goat.

"Dear sirs," they said, "maybe you can help us."

"And what has happened to you?" asked Nitechka.

"Deluge and destruction threaten us. Our King died a week ago, and since that time a terrible rain has come down upon our gorgeous town. We can't even make fires in our houses, because so much water runs through the chimneys. We will perish, honorable sirs!"

"It is too bad," said Nitechka very wisely.

"Oh, very bad! And we are most sorry for the late King's daughter. The poor thing can't stop crying, and this causes even more water."

"That makes it still worse," replied Nitechka, still more wisely.

"Help us, help us!" continued the burgomaster. "Do you know the immeasurable reward the Princess promises to the one who stops the rain? She promises to marry him, and then he will become King."

"Truly?" cried Nitechka. "Count Scarecrow, let's go to the town. We ought to try to help them."

Through the terrible rain they were led to the Princess. Upon seeing Nitechka, she cried out:

"Oh, what a handsome youth!"

He hopped three times and said:

"Is it true, Princess, that you will marry the one who stops the rain?"

"I vowed I would."

"And if I do it?"

"I will keep my promise."

"And I shall become a King?"

"You will, O beautiful youth."

"Very well," answered the tailor. "I am going to stop the rain."

So saying, he nodded to Count Scarecrow and they left the Princess.

The whole population, full of hope, gathered around them.

Nitechka and the scarecrow stood under an umbrella and whispered to each other:

"Listen, Scarecrow, what shall we do to make the rain stop falling?"

"We have to bring back pleasant weather."

"But how?"

"Ha! Let's think!"

But for three days they thought, and the rain fell and fell and fell. Suddenly Nitechka gave a cry of joy like a goat's bleating.

"I know where the rain comes from!"

"Where from?"

"From the sky!"

"Eh!" grumbled the scarecrow. "I know that too. Surely it doesn't fall from the bottom to the top, but the other way around."

"Yes," said Nitechka, "but why does it always fall over the town only, and not ever elsewhere?"

"Because elsewhere there is nice weather."

"You're stupid, Mr. Count," said the tailor. "But tell me, how long has it rained?"

"They say since the King died."

"You see! Now I know everything! The King was so great and mighty that when he died and went to heaven, he made a huge hole in the sky."

"Oh, oh, true!"

"Through the hole the rain poured and it will pour until the end of the world if the hole isn't sewn up!"

Count Scarecrow looked at him in amazement.

"In all my life I have never seen such a wise tailor," said he.

They rejoiced greatly, went to the burgomaster, and ordered him to tell the townspeople that Mr. Joseph Nitechka, a citizen of the town of Taidaraida, had promised to stop the rain.

"Long live Mr. Nitechka! Long may he live!" shouted the whole town.

Nitechka ordered them to bring all the ladders in the town, tie them together, and lean them against the sky. He took a hundred needles and, threading one, went up the ladders. Count Scarecrow stayed at the bottom and unwound the spool on which there were a hundred miles of thread.

When Nitechka got to the very top, he saw that there was a huge hole in the sky, a hole as big as the town. A torn piece of the sky hung down, and through this hole the water poured.

So he went to work and sewed and sewed for two days. His fingers grew stiff and he became very tired, but he did not stop. When he had finished sewing, he pressed out the sky with the iron and then, exhausted, went down the ladders.

Once more the sun shone over Pacanów. Count Scarecrow almost went mad with joy, as did all the other inhabitants of the town. The Princess wiped her eyes that were almost cried out. Throwing herself on Nitechka's neck, she kissed him affectionately.

Nitechka was very happy. He looked around. There were the burgomaster and councilmen bringing him a golden scepter and a gorgeous crown, and shouting:

"Long live King Nitechka! Long live he! Long live he! And let him be the Princess's husband, and let him reign happily!"

So the merry little tailor reigned happily for a long time, and the rain never fell in his kingdom. In his good fortune Nitechka did not forget his old friend, Count Scarecrow. He appointed him the Great Warden of the Kingdom, to drive away the sparrows from the royal head.

Russia

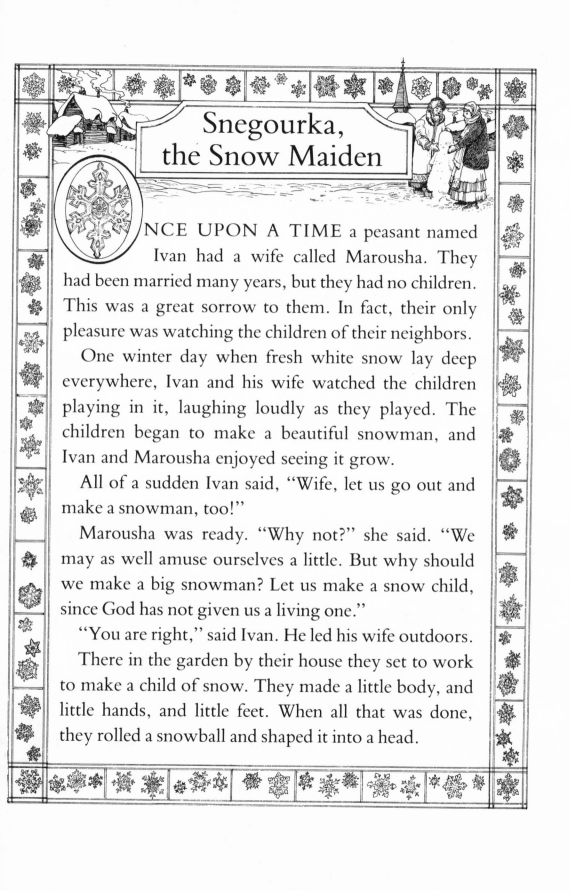

Snegourka, the Snow Maiden

ONCE UPON A TIME a peasant named Ivan had a wife called Marousha. They had been married many years, but they had no children. This was a great sorrow to them. In fact, their only pleasure was watching the children of their neighbors.

One winter day when fresh white snow lay deep everywhere, Ivan and his wife watched the children playing in it, laughing loudly as they played. The children began to make a beautiful snowman, and Ivan and Marousha enjoyed seeing it grow.

All of a sudden Ivan said, "Wife, let us go out and make a snowman, too!"

Marousha was ready. "Why not?" she said. "We may as well amuse ourselves a little. But why should we make a big snowman? Let us make a snow child, since God has not given us a living one."

"You are right," said Ivan. He led his wife outdoors.

There in the garden by their house they set to work to make a child of snow. They made a little body, and little hands, and little feet. When all that was done, they rolled a snowball and shaped it into a head.

"Heaven bless you!" cried a passerby.

"Thanks," replied Ivan.

"The help of heaven is always good," said Marousha.

"What are you doing?" asked the passerby.

"Look," said Ivan.

"We are making a snow girl," said Marousha.

On the ball of snow that stood for a head they put a nose and a chin, and they made two little holes for eyes.

Just as they finished their work – oh, wonderful! – the little snow maiden moved! Ivan felt a warm breath come from her lips. He drew back and looked. The snow maiden's sparkling eyes were blue. Her lips, rosy now, curved in a lovely smile.

"What is this?" cried Ivan, making the sign of the cross.

The snow maiden bent her head and the snow fell from now golden hair, which curled about her soft round cheeks. She moved her little arms and legs in the snow as if she were a real child.

"Ivan! Ivan!" cried Marousha. "Heaven has heard our prayers." She threw herself on the child and covered her with kisses.

"Ah, Snegourka, my own dear snow maiden," she cried, and she carried her into the house.

Ivan had much to do to recover from his surprise. Marousha became foolish with joy.

Hour by hour, Snegourka, the snow maiden, grew both in size and in beauty. Ivan and Marousha could not take their eyes away from her.

The little house, which had held such sadness, now was full of life and merriment. The neighboring children came to play with the little snow maiden. They chattered with her and sang songs to her, teaching her all they knew.

The snow maiden was very clever. She noticed everything and learned quickly. When she spoke, her voice was so sweet that one could have gone on listening to it forever. She was gentle, obedient, and loving. In turn, everyone loved her. She played in the snow with the others and they saw how well her little hands could model things of snow and ice.

Marousha said, "See what joy heaven has given us in our old age."

"Heaven be thanked," replied Ivan.

At last the winter came to an end, and the spring sun shone down and warmed the earth. The snow melted, green grass sprang up in the fields, and the lark sang high in the sky. The village girls went singing:

"Sweet spring, how did you come to us?
How did you come?
Did you come on a plow, or on a harrow?"

Although the other children were gay with spring, and full of song and dance, the snow maiden sat by the window, looking more and more sad.

"What is the matter with you, my dear child?" asked Marousha, drawing her close and caressing her. "Are you not well? You are not merry."

"It is nothing, Mother," answered the snow maiden. "I am quite well."

The last snow of the winter had now melted and disappeared. Flowers bloomed in every field and garden. In the forest, the nightingale poured out its song and all the world seemed glad, except the snow maiden, who became still sadder.

She would run away from her friends and hide from the sun in dark nooks, like a timid flower under the trees. She liked best to play by the water, under shady willow trees. She was happy at night and during a storm, even during a fierce hailstorm. When the sun broke forth again – when the hail melted – she began to weep.

Summer came, with ripening fields, and the Feast of Saint John was at hand. The snow maiden's friends begged her to go with them to the forest, to pick berries and flowers.

The snow maiden did not want to go, but her mother urged her, even though she, too, felt afraid.

"Go, my child, and play. And you, her friends, look well after her. You know how much I love her."

In the forest the children picked wild flowers and made themselves wreaths. It was warm, and they ran about singing, each wearing a crown of flowers.

"Look at us," they said to the snow maiden. "Look how we run! Follow us."

They went on, dancing and singing. Then all of a sudden they heard, behind them, a sigh. . . .

They looked. There was nothing to be seen. They looked again. The snow maiden was no longer among them.

They called out and shouted her name, but there was no answer.

"Where can she be? She must have gone home," they said.

Back they ran to the village, but no one there had seen her either.

During the next day and the day following, everyone searched. They went through the woods and looked through every thicket, but no trace of the little snow maiden was to be found.

Ivan and Marousha felt their hearts were broken. For a long

time Marousha would cry, "Snegourka, my sweet snow maiden, come to me!"

Sometimes Ivan and Marousha thought they could hear the voice of their child. Perhaps, when the snow returned, she would come back to them.

The Flying Ship

ONCE UPON A TIME a man and his wife had three sons. Two sons were clever, but the third was a fool. The old woman loved the first two, and quite spoiled them, but she gave little of anything to the third.

One day a message came from the Tsar that said, "Whoever builds a ship that can fly, to him will I give my daughter, the Tsarevna, in marriage."

The elder brothers said at once that they must go and seek their fortunes, and they begged a blessing of their parents. Their mother got them ready for the journey, filling their packs with the best of food to eat on the way, and the best to drink, too.

The fool then began to beg to go, too. But his mother asked, "Where would *you* go, fool? Why, the wolves would devour you!"

But the fool kept insisting, "I will go, I will go!" Finally his mother saw that she could do nothing with him, so she gave him a piece of dry bread and a flask of water, and shoved him out of the house.

The fool went on and on. At last he met an old man, and they stopped to greet each other.

The old man asked the fool, "Where are you going?"

"Well, now!" said the fool, all excited. "The Tsar has promised to give his daughter to anyone who can make a ship that can fly."

"And can you make such a ship?"

"No, I cannot, but somewhere I will get it made."

"And where is that somewhere?"

"Heaven only knows."

"Well, now, sit down. Rest and eat a bit. Take out what you have in your knapsack."

"Oh, but it is such poor food that I am ashamed to show it."

"Nonsense! Take it out! What God has given is quite good enough."

The fool undid his knapsack. He could not believe his eyes! There, instead of the dry crust of bread, lay soft white rolls and savory meats. Gladly he shared them with the old man.

So they ate together, and the old man said to the fool, "Go into the wood, right up to the first tree, and cross yourself three times. Next you must strike the tree with your ax, fall with your face to the ground, and wait until someone wakes you. Then you will see before you a ship. You may sit in it and fly wherever you like. But be sure to take on board anyone you meet on your way!"

The fool blessed the old man and said farewell. Going into the wood, he went right up to the first tree and did exactly as he had been told. He crossed himself three times before he

struck the tree with his ax. Then he lay down with his face to the ground and went to sleep.

In a little while someone woke him and he sat up. There before him was a ship! Without thinking long about it, the fool climbed in. Up into the air the ship rose, and it flew on and on.

When the fool looked down, on the road below he saw a man lying with his ear to the damp earth.

"Good day, Uncle!"

"Good day."

"What are you doing?"

"I am listening to what is going on in the world."

"Do come and fly in the ship with me."

The Listener did not want to refuse, so he climbed aboard. On and on the two flew together.

Soon they looked down to the ground. There they saw a man hopping along on one leg, with the other tied tightly to his ear.

"Good day, Uncle. Why are you hopping on one leg?"

"Why, if I were to untie the other, I could be halfway around the world in a single stride."

"Do come and fly with us."

Swift-of-Foot climbed aboard, and they flew on and on.

Again they looked below. There they saw a man standing with a gun and taking aim.

"Good day, Uncle. At what are you aiming? There is not a bird in sight."

"What! I could hit a bird or beast a hundred leagues away. That's what I call shooting!"

"Please come and fly with us." The Marksman joined them, and they flew on and on.

Once more they looked down. Now they saw a man carrying on his back a whole sackload of bread.

"Good day, Uncle. Where are you going?"

"I am going to get some bread for dinner."

"But you've got a whole sackload on your back."

"That! Why, I could eat all that in a single mouthful."

"Do come and fly with us."

The Gobbler climbed aboard, and they went flying on and on.

When they looked down now they saw a man walking around a lake.

"Good day, Uncle. What are you looking for?"

"I want to drink, but I can find no water."

"But there's a whole lake before you. Why don't you have a drink of it?"

"That! Why, that water would not be more than a mouthful to me."

"Then do come and fly with us."

The Drinker climbed aboard, and they flew on and on.

Again they looked down. There was a man walking into the forest, and on his shoulders he carried a bundle of wood.

"Good day, Uncle. Why are you taking wood to the forest?"

"This is not common wood."

"What sort of wood is it, then?"

"It is so remarkable that if you scatter pieces of this wood, a whole army will spring up."

"Do fly with us then."

The Wood-gatherer joined them, and they flew on and on.

They looked down once more, and this time they saw a man carrying a sack of straw.

"Good day, Uncle. Where are you carrying that straw?"

"To the village."

"Is there no straw in the village, then?"

"Yes, but this is rare and wonderful straw. If you scatter it on the hottest summer day, the day will become cold at once with snow and frost."

"Won't you fly with us, then?"

"Thank you, I will," said the Straw-carrier.

Soon they flew into the courtyard of the Tsar's palace. The Tsar was dining just then, but he heard the flying ship. He was much surprised! He sent his servant out to ask who was flying that ship. The servant brought back word that it was only a poor peasant.

The Tsar fell to thinking. He did not like the idea of giving his lovely daughter to a simple peasant, and so he began to consider how he could settle with him. He decided, "I will give him many impossible tasks to do."

Immediately the Tsar had a servant order the fool to bring him, as soon as the imperial meal was over, some singing water from the end of the world.

Now, the first man whom the fool had met (the one who had been listening to what was going on in the world) heard what the Tsar was saying to the servant, and told it to the fool.

"What shall I do now?" asked the fool. "Why, if I should search for a year, and even for my whole life, I would never find such water."

"Don't be afraid," said Swift-of-Foot, his second friend. "I'll manage it for you."

The servant came and made known the Tsar's command.

"Tell the Tsar I shall fetch the water," replied the fool.

Swift-of-Foot untied his other leg from his ear and ran off. In a twinkling he came to the end of the world, where he found the singing water.

"I must make haste to return," said he. But, instead, he sat down under a water mill and went to sleep.

The Tsar's dinner was drawing to a close. Still Swift-of-Foot did not return, and those on board the ship grew uneasy.

The Listener lay down, ear to the ground. "Oh, ho! So you are asleep beneath the mill, are you?"

The Marksman took up his gun. He aimed at the mill and awoke Swift-of-Foot with his shooting.

Swift-of-Foot ran, and in a moment brought the water, just before the Tsar rose from his table.

But the singing water was not enough to satisfy the Tsar. He bade his servant say to the fool, "Come. Since you are so clever, show me that you and your comrades can eat at one meal twenty roasted oxen and twenty loaves of bread."

Listener heard this and told it to the fool.

The fool was terrified. "Why, I can't eat even one loaf at a meal!"

"Don't be afraid," said Gobbler. "That will be very little for me."

The servant came and gave the Tsar's command.

"Good!" said the fool. "Let us have the food and we'll eat it."

The Tsar's men then brought twenty roasted oxen, and twenty loaves of bread.

Gobbler, alone, ate it all!

"Ugh!" he said. "Precious little. They might have given us a *little* more!"

Now the Tsar ordered the fool to drink forty barrels of wine. Each barrel was to hold forty buckets.

The Listener heard these words, and told them to the fool.

The fool was horrified. "Why, I could not drink even one bucketful!"

"Don't be frightened," said the Drinker. "I'll drink for all. It will be little enough for me."

The Tsar's men poured out forty barrels of wine. The Drinker came and swallowed it all at one gulp. "Ugh! Little enough, too," he said. "I should have liked as much more again."

After that the Tsar commanded the fool to go to the bathhouse to make himself ready for his wedding.

Now this bathhouse was made of cast iron, and the Tsar commanded that it should be heated scalding hot. He intended that the fool should be boiled in a single instant.

The fool was frightened. But as he went into the bathhouse, the Straw-carrier followed him. They were both locked in.

Now the fool's friend scattered his straw, and at once the water in the bath froze so hard that the fool was scarcely able to wash himself. He crept up onto the stove and spent the night there.

In the morning when the servants unlocked the bathhouse, they found the fool alive and well, lying on the stove and singing happily.

The Tsar was puzzled. He did not know how to rid himself of this fool. He thought and thought. At last he commanded the fool to collect a whole army of his own soldiers – for, thought he, "How will a simple peasant be able to form an army? Certainly he will not be able to do *that*."

The fool heard this new command with alarm. "Now I am lost," said he. "You have saved me more than once, my friends, but it is plain that you can do nothing now."

"You're a fine fellow," said the man with the bundle of wood. "Why, you've forgotten all about me, haven't you?"

The servant came and gave the fool the Tsar's command.

"If you will have his daughter, you must have a whole army on foot by morning."

"I agree," said the fool. "But if the Tsar, even after this, should refuse, I will conquer his whole kingdom and take his daughter by force."

At night the Wood-gatherer went out into the fields. He began scattering his sticks in all directions. Immediately a great army sprang up, some on horse and some on foot.

In the morning, the Tsar saw the army standing on all sides.

Now it was his turn to be terrified. Without wasting a minute, he had his men carry gifts of rare gems and fine clothing to the fool. And he ordered his men to bring the fool to court. He would marry him to the Tsarevna.

The fool attired himself in the costly garments, which made him more handsome than words can describe. Then he came before the Tsar.

And he married the beautiful Tsarevna, who came to love him as he loved her, and they lived together happily for many long years.

Scotland

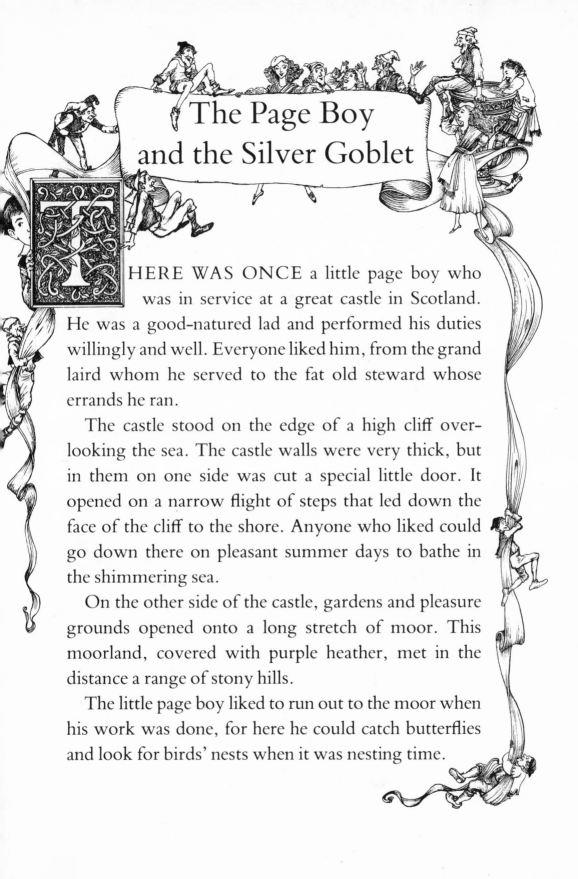

The Page Boy and the Silver Goblet

THERE WAS ONCE a little page boy who was in service at a great castle in Scotland. He was a good-natured lad and performed his duties willingly and well. Everyone liked him, from the grand laird whom he served to the fat old steward whose errands he ran.

The castle stood on the edge of a high cliff overlooking the sea. The castle walls were very thick, but in them on one side was cut a special little door. It opened on a narrow flight of steps that led down the face of the cliff to the shore. Anyone who liked could go down there on pleasant summer days to bathe in the shimmering sea.

On the other side of the castle, gardens and pleasure grounds opened onto a long stretch of moor. This moorland, covered with purple heather, met in the distance a range of stony hills.

The little page boy liked to run out to the moor when his work was done, for here he could catch butterflies and look for birds' nests when it was nesting time.

The old steward himself was glad to have the lad play there. But before the boy went out, the old man always warned him:

"Now, mind my words, laddie, and keep far away from the Fairy Knowe, for you cannot trust the Little Folk."

This Knowe was a rocky green hillock, which stood on the moor not twenty yards from the garden gate. People said that it was the home of fairies. And everyone knew that the fairies would punish any rash mortal who came too near them. Because of this the country folk would walk a good half-mile out of their way, even in daylight, to avoid going too near the Fairy Knowe. At night they would hardly step on the moor; for then, as everyone knows, the fairies come abroad in the darkness. And they leave the door of their dwelling open, so that an unlucky mortal who does not take care may find himself inside.

Now the little page boy, instead of being frightened of the fairies, was anxious to see them. He wanted to visit their home, just to find out what it was like.

One night, when everyone else was asleep, he crept out of the castle by the little side door. He stole down the stone steps and along the shore. Up on the moor, he went straight to the Fairy Knowe.

To his delight he found that what everyone said was true. The top of the rocky Knowe was tipped up, and from this opening rays of light streamed out.

His heart beat fast with excitement as, gathering his courage, he stooped down and slipped inside the Knowe.

He found himself in a large room lit by hundreds of tiny candles. Around a polished table sat scores of the Little People. They were dressed in green, and yellow, and pink; in blue, and lilac, and scarlet – in all the colors possible.

The page boy stood in a dark corner watching, in wonder, a busy scene of feasting. How strange that here, within sight of the castle, all these tiny beings were living their lives unknown to men!

Suddenly someone gave an order.

"Fetch the cup!" cried a shrill voice. Instantly two fairy pages, in scarlet livery, darted from the table to a tiny cupboard in the rock. They returned staggering under the weight of a beautiful silver cup. Richly embossed it was, and lined with shining gold.

Up to the middle of the table they lifted the cup. Then, with clapping of hands and shouts of joy, all the fairies began in turn to drink from it.

The page boy could see, from where he stood, that although no one poured wine into the goblet, it was always full. Also, he saw that the drink was not always of the same kind. Each fairy, when he grasped the goblet's stem, wished for the drink that he loved best; and lo! in a moment the cup became full.

"It would be a fine thing if I could show that cup at the castle," thought the page boy. "No one will believe that I have been here unless I have something to show for it." He bided his time and watched.

Presently the fairies noticed the page boy. Instead of being angry at him for entering their dwelling, as he had expected they would be, they seemed pleased to see him. They even invited him to a seat at their feast.

Later, however, they became rude. They jeered at him for being content to serve mere mortals, and told him that they saw everything that went on at the castle. They made fun of the fat old steward, whom the page boy loved with all his heart. They laughed at the castle food, saying that it was fit only for animals. When the scarlet-clad pages set a fresh dainty on their table, the fairies pushed the dish across to the boy, saying, "Taste this, for you cannot eat such things at the castle."

At last the page boy could stand their teasing no longer. Besides, he knew that if he wanted to secure the cup he must lose no time.

Suddenly he stood up. Tightly he grasped the stem of the silver goblet. "I'll drink to you all in water," he cried. Instantly, the ruby wine was turned to clear, cold water.

He raised the cup to his lips, but he did not drink from it. With a sudden jerk he threw the water over the candles. Instantly the room was in darkness. Clasping the precious cup tightly in his arms, he sprang to the opening of the Knowe, through which he could see the stars glimmering.

Soon the page boy was speeding over the wet, dew-spangled moor, with the whole troop of fairies at his heels. They were wild with rage and uttered shrill shouts of fury. The page boy knew well that, if they should overtake him, he would have no mercy at their hands.

His heart began to sink, for, fleet of foot though he was, he was no match for the Little Folk. They gained on him steadily.

All seemed lost, when a strange voice sounded out of the darkness:

"If thou wouldst gain the castle door,
Keep to the black stones on the shore."

It was the voice of some poor mortal who had been taken by the fairies and who did not want a like fate to befall the brave page boy.

This made the page boy remember a saying he had heard: *He who walks on wet sands, which the waves have washed, the fairies cannot touch.*

The page boy turned and dashed, panting, down to the

shore. At first, his feet sank in dry sand. His breath came in little gasps, and he felt as if he must give up his struggle. But he pushed on; and at last, just as the first of the fairies was about to lay hands on him, he made a long jump. He landed on wet sand from which the waves had just receded, and he knew that he was safe.

The Little Folk could go not one step farther. They had to remain on the dry sand, shrieking with cries of rage and disappointment.

The triumphant page boy ran safely along the shore, with the precious cup in his arms. He climbed lightly up the steps in the rock, and disappeared through the little door.

For many years, long after the page boy had grown up and become a stately steward who trained other page boys, the beautiful cup remained in the castle. It was a witness to his adventure in outwitting the fairies.

The Brownie o' Ferne-Den

MANY BROWNIES there have been in Scotland. And one of them was known as "the Brownie o' Ferne-Den."

Now, Ferne-Den was a farmhouse. It had its name from the glen, or "den," near which it stood, for anyone who wished to reach the farm had to pass through this glen.

All around, the country folk believed that a brownie lived in the glen. Never would he appear to anyone in the daytime, but it was said he was sometimes seen at night. He would steal about like an ungainly shadow, moving from tree to tree to keep from being seen. And he never did harm to anybody, this Brownie o' Ferne-Den.

Indeed, like all good brownies that are properly treated and let alone, the Brownie o' Ferne-Den was always on the lookout to do a good turn to those in need of his help.

The farmer of Ferne-Den did not know what he would ever do without this brownie. If he had any farmwork to be finished in a hurry, it would be done. The brownie would thrash his grain, and winnow it, and tie it up into bags. He would cut the turnips, too. And for the farmer's wife he would wash the clothes, work the churn, or weed the garden.

All that the farmer and his wife had to do was to leave open the door of the barn, or the turnip shed, or the milkhouse, when they went to bed. And they must put down a bowl of new milk on the doorstep for the brownie's supper. When they woke the next morning the bowl would be empty, and the job would be finished better than if it had been done by mortal hands.

Now, all of this should have proved how gentle and kindly this brownie was. But all the workers on the farm had a fear of him. They would go miles around in the dark, coming home from kirk on the Sunday or market on Market Day, to avoid passing through the brownie's glen and catching a sight of him.

The farmer's lady herself was so good and gentle a housewife that she felt no fear of the brownie. When the brownie's supper was to be left outside, it was she who would fill his bowl with the richest milk, and she would add a good spoonful of cream to it, too.

"Aye," said she, "he works hard for us, right enough, and never asks for wages. Well does he deserve the very best meal we can set out for him."

One night this gentle lady was taken ill, and everyone was afraid she might die. Her husband took it hard, indeed, and so, too, did her servants. Such a good mistress she had ever been to them that they loved her as if she were their mother. Now she was that bad that they were all for sending for the old nurse, who lived miles off on the other side of the glen.

Who was to go to fetch her? That was the question. It was black midnight when the lady fell ill, and the only way to the old nurse's house lay straight through the glen. Whoever traveled that road would run the risk of meeting the brownie.

The farmer himself would have gone, well enough, but he dared not leave his wife. As for the timid servants, they stood about in the kitchen, each telling the other that he was the one to go. And no one of them offered to go himself.

Little did they know that the brownie, who was the very cause of their fear, was hiding only a few feet away from them, in the entry outside the kitchen. There he crouched, a queer wee man, all covered with hair. He had a long beard and red-rimmed eyes. His broad feet were webbed like those of a duck, and his long arms touched the ground, even when he stood up.

The brownie, with his face all anxious, tried to hear their words. He had come as usual from his home in the glen to see if there was any work for him to do, and to look for his bowl of milk. He knew fine that something now was wrong inside the farmhouse. Usually, at this late hour, all was dark and still, but here were the windows lit up and the door wide open.

The brownie learned from the servants' jabber that his kind mistress, whom he loved so dearly, was deathly ill. He became

sad, indeed. And when he found that the silly servants were so full of their fears that they dared not go for the nurse, his anger grew far greater than their fear.

"Fools and idiots!" he muttered, stamping his queer flat feet. "They talk as if a brownie would take a bite right off them. If the like of them only knew the bother they give me to keep out of *their* way, they would not be so silly. Aye, by my troth, if they keep on like this, the bonny lady will die amongst their fingers. It strikes me that brownie must away, himself, for the nurse."

Up he reached with his hand and took down from its peg on the wall the farmer's great dark cloak. Hiding under it, he hurried out to the stable, to saddle and bridle the farmer's fleetest horse.

When the last buckle was fastened, the brownie led the horse out of the stable and scrambled up onto its back. "If ever you have flown fast, fly fast now," begged the brownie.

It was as if the horse understood the brownie. It gave a quick whinny, pricked up its ears, and darted into the darkness like an arrow from a bow.

In less time than the distance had ever been traveled before, the brownie came to the old woman's cottage.

Now the nurse, of course, was in bed asleep. The brownie had to rap sharply on her window. When she rose and put her old face close to the glass to ask who was there, he told her quickly why he had come at this late hour.

"You must come with me, Goodwife, and that at once," he commanded in a deep voice, "if the lady of Ferne-Den is to be saved. There is no one to nurse her at the farm save the lot of silly servants."

"Aye, but how shall I get there? Have they sent a cart for me?" asked the old woman. As far as she could see, there was nothing at the door save the horse and its rider.

"Nay, they have sent no cart," replied the brownie. "You must just climb up behind me on the saddle, and hang on tight. I'll promise to land you at Ferne-Den safe and sound."

The brownie's voice was so commanding that the old woman dared not refuse to do as she was bid. Besides, she had often ridden thus on a horse when she was a lassie. So, she made haste to dress herself and soon unlocked her door. She climbed up behind the stranger, who was almost hidden in his dark cloak. She clasped him tightly and they were off.

Not a word was spoken between them till they neared the glen. Then the old woman began to feel her courage giving way. "Do you think we might meet the brownie?" she asked timidly. "I have no fancy to run the risk, for folk say that he is an unchancy creature."

The brownie gave his own odd laugh. "Keep up your heart,

and cease talking foolishly," he said. "I promise you there will be naught uglier this night than the man you ride behind."

"Oh, good on you, then, I'm fine and safe," said the old woman. "I have not seen your face, but I warrant you are a true man, for the care you have taken of the poor lady of Ferne-Den."

She fell into silence again till they had passed through the glen and the good horse had turned into the farmyard. The brownie now slid to the ground. Turning around, he carefully lifted her down with his long, strong arms. But – as he did so, the cloak slipped off him. She saw his strange, short body.

"In all the world, what kind of man are you?" the old woman asked. She peered into his face in the graying light of morning. "What makes your eyes so big? And what have you done to your feet? They are more like duck's webs than aught else."

The queer little brownie laughed. "I've walked many a mile without a horse to help me, and I've heard it said that too much walking makes the feet unshapely.

"But waste no time in talking now, good dame. Go into the house. And if anyone asks who brought you hither so quickly, tell them – they who fear the brownie – that there was a lack of men to help the good mistress. You had to ride here behind the BROWNIE O' FERNE-DEN."

Spain

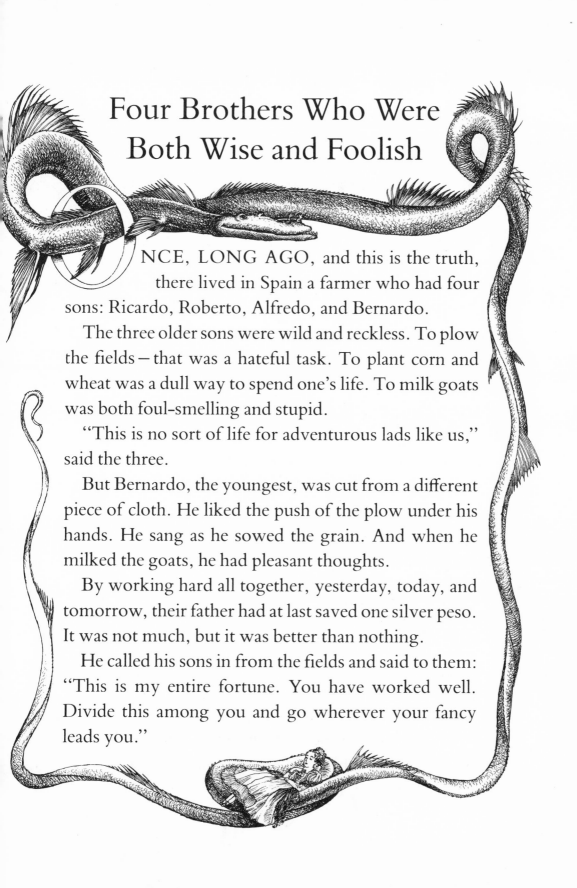

Four Brothers Who Were Both Wise and Foolish

ONCE, LONG AGO, and this is the truth, there lived in Spain a farmer who had four sons: Ricardo, Roberto, Alfredo, and Bernardo.

The three older sons were wild and reckless. To plow the fields – that was a hateful task. To plant corn and wheat was a dull way to spend one's life. To milk goats was both foul-smelling and stupid.

"This is no sort of life for adventurous lads like us," said the three.

But Bernardo, the youngest, was cut from a different piece of cloth. He liked the push of the plow under his hands. He sang as he sowed the grain. And when he milked the goats, he had pleasant thoughts.

By working hard all together, yesterday, today, and tomorrow, their father had at last saved one silver peso. It was not much, but it was better than nothing.

He called his sons in from the fields and said to them: "This is my entire fortune. You have worked well. Divide this among you and go wherever your fancy leads you."

The four lads split the peso into quarter-pieces. Each put one in his pocket.

"Now we can seek our fortunes," said Ricardo.

"After that we will seek adventures," said Roberto.

"One of us must marry a King's daughter," said Alfredo.

But Bernardo shook his head. "I don't care much about doing any of those things. I had far rather stay at home."

His brothers scoffed. They called him a fool. They called him a silly fellow, a buffoon. They said he did not know when he was well off.

So, when they took their departure, Bernardo went with them. Hay foot, straw foot, each followed his brother's heels until they came to a place where four roads crossed. Here they halted.

"Let us separate now," said Ricardo. "Let each of us follow his own road and find what fortune awaits him. At the end of a year, we will meet here. Is it agreed?"

"Agreed," said Roberto and Alfredo.

But Bernardo shook his head: "I don't care about going any farther. I'd rather go home."

But the others pulled him about, and called him a simpleton.

"I will take the road going north," said Ricardo.

"I will take the road going east," said Roberto.

"And I – the road south," said Alfredo.

That left for Bernardo the road going west. He took it with small comfort and tramped off without looking back.

On the road north, Ricardo was set upon by a band of robbers. They tied him to a donkey, after they took his quarter-piece of peso and beat him for having so little wealth. Then they bore him off to their hideaway in the mountains.

In six months their leader died. Ricardo by now had shown himself so reckless and clever that they made him chief of the band.

On the road going east, Roberto traded his silver for an old gun. By performing a trick here and another there, he managed to keep himself in food and his gun in bullets. He practiced shooting all day and every day, until his marksmanship became so perfect that he could clip the smallest leaf from its tree a half-mile away.

On the road south, Alfredo overtook a small man wearing enormous spectacles.

"Your glasses fit you badly," said Alfredo, "and what are you looking at?"

"Not much," said the man. "Just taking a look at China. They are having a great flood there."

"Marvelous," said Alfredo.

"Tiresome," said the small man. "When you look at China, you forget Spain. When you look inside a house in Persia, you forget there is a cozy little house waiting for you in Andalusia. I have grown rich seeing too much. Now I think I will go home and look no farther than the walls around my patio. You can have the spectacles for whatever you happen to have in your pocket."

"Agreed," said Alfredo.

And he gave the small man his quarter-piece of peso.

Bernardo, the youngest brother, wandered a day and a night

along his road and found nothing. He was about to turn back, when he came across a coppersmith's shop.

All that second day he watched the coppersmith mending kettles, fitting copper bands about great casks, making pots and ladles and all sorts of useful things.

"If I can't be a farmer," he thought, "I will become a coppersmith." So he gave the fellow his quarter-piece to teach him his trade.

At the end of the year the four brothers met at the crossroads.

"I have become a robber chief. Anything in the world that I like I can take for my own," said Ricardo.

"I have become the greatest marksman in Spain," said Roberto, showing off his fowling-piece. "Show me the smallest object at the farthest distance, and I can hit it."

Alfredo put on his spectacles. "I can see the Emperor of China sitting down to tea in his garden and a fly that is crawling on his nose."

Bernardo hung his head. He could not look his fine brothers in the eye.

"Come, speak up, stupid one," said the others. "What have you to show for your year?"

"Nothing worth talking about. I am just a poor coppersmith. I can mend a pot or a kettle – that is all. Now let us go home."

The others laughed till their sides ached, calling him a goose – a simpleton – a buffoon – the worst one in all of Spain. "If we let you go home now you would remain a simpleton all your life. You shall come with us on our adventure."

Alfredo looked all around the world to see in what direction adventure might lie. "Oh-oh!" he said at last, and pointed to the east. "Yonder lies the sea. On the sea lies an island. On the island sleeps a captive Princess, guarded night and day by a giant sea serpent."

"We will rescue her!" shouted Ricardo.

"Agreed!" shouted Roberto and Alfredo.

Bernardo shook his head. "I don't care much about sea serpents, or rescuing a Princess. I'd rather go home."

But the others pulled him along. And before he knew it, they were looking across the sea. They fitted up a small vessel and set sail for the island. How many days they sailed does not matter. They reached there in the dark of dawn.

Alfredo put on his spectacles and looked. "The serpent sleeps," said he. "But he is coiled around the Princess to the height of the tower."

"Does the Princess sleep?" asked Bernardo.

"Of course she sleeps. What has that to do with it?" Alfredo was scornful.

"A sleeping Princess is not apt to scream. A screaming Princess could waken a sea serpent. Let us have our coffee first."

For once the others agreed. They had their coffee. Then Ricardo was put softly ashore.

"Watch me," he whispered. "Now I will steal the Princess, for that is my profession."

Everything went well until the last moment. Then Ricardo

caught his foot on the serpent's tail. That woke him and he gave a great roar. That woke the Princess and she screamed. That set Ricardo running, hot for the beach. He swam and the serpent swam. Ricardo boarded the ship and set down the Princess. The serpent came close, very close.

"Now," said Roberto, "I will shoot the serpent, for that is my profession."

Shoot him he did, clean through the middle. But the serpent gave three dying lashes with the end of his tail. *Flip-flap-flop!* It cut the ship nearly in two. The three brothers and the Princess were terrified, for drowning looked very near.

"There is nothing to be scared of," said Bernardo. "Mending is my profession." He proceeded to get his tools and some long strips of copper and he welded the two parts of the ship together until she was as good as new. "Safe and snug," said he.

They lifted anchor and sailed to the country where the Princess's father was King. I cannot tell you if it was Greece or Persia or Asia. All I know is that the ship got there.

The King was enormously pleased to have his daughter rescued. He had been too busy with affairs of state to do it himself. And he was more than willing to reward the one who had done it. He would do it very handsomely – not only with the Princess herself, but with a large sack of gold as well.

"I rescued her," said Alfredo. And when the others looked surprised, he added, "Had I not put on my spectacles and discovered her, she would still be on the island."

"I rescued her," said Ricardo. "Didn't I steal her from the middle of the serpent's coils?"

"And stepped on his tail and woke him," reminded Roberto. "Had I not shot the serpent, where would we all be? Dead!"

The King listened solemnly. Then he pointed a finger at Bernardo: "*You* – what did you do?"

"Nothing much," said Bernardo. "When the serpent cut the ship in two, I mended it."

"Then *you* rescued the Princess." The King said it with such kingly authority that no one dared dispute him. "You shall marry the Princess."

Bernardo shook his head. "I don't care much about being the husband of a Princess," he said. "I would rather go home."

"Come, come!" said the King.

"Come, come!" said the brothers.

"Come," said the Princess. "I'll go with you. I've always wanted to milk a goat."

So they all separated. Ricardo took the road north and went back to his robber band. Roberto took his gun and went east. Alfredo put on his spectacles and stepped high into the south. But Bernardo and the Princess went west, singing all the way home.

Juan Cigarron

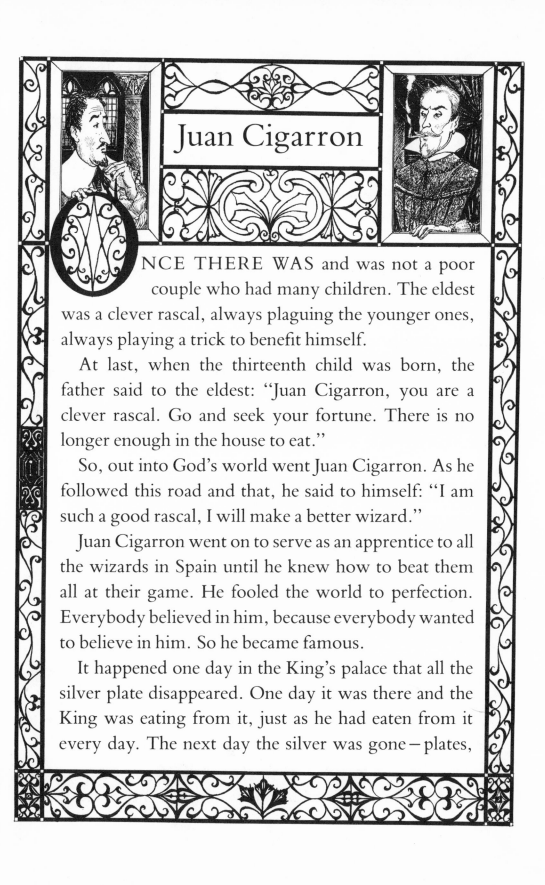

ONCE THERE WAS and was not a poor couple who had many children. The eldest was a clever rascal, always plaguing the younger ones, always playing a trick to benefit himself.

At last, when the thirteenth child was born, the father said to the eldest: "Juan Cigarron, you are a clever rascal. Go and seek your fortune. There is no longer enough in the house to eat."

So, out into God's world went Juan Cigarron. As he followed this road and that, he said to himself: "I am such a good rascal, I will make a better wizard."

Juan Cigarron went on to serve as an apprentice to all the wizards in Spain until he knew how to beat them all at their game. He fooled the world to perfection. Everybody believed in him, because everybody wanted to believe in him. So he became famous.

It happened one day in the King's palace that all the silver plate disappeared. One day it was there and the King was eating from it, just as he had eaten from it every day. The next day the silver was gone – plates, goblets, trenchers, and tankards – as if the earth had swallowed them.

"Send for Juan Cigarron," said the King. "I have heard that he is the greatest wizard in Spain. I believe that he may be the greatest *rascal*. We shall try him."

So a messenger was sent and Juan Cigarron was brought to the palace, straight to the hall where the King sat eating from a common clay dish.

"The royal silver is gone – stolen. You are to find it, and learn who stole it," said the King. "But you shall make your discovery while locked in the deepest dungeon in the palace. Being a great wizard, you can do your work there as well as anywhere else. If you should turn out to be a cheating rascal, instead of a wizard, we will have you there – safe, hide and hair – to hang, as a fine example. Three days now you shall have to find the royal silver."

The guards led Juan Cigarron to the dungeon. They fastened an iron ball and chain to his feet. They locked him in with a key as large as his leg bone. They left him alone all day that he might better practice his magic, and all day his heart grew heavier.

"I am well caught," thought Juan Cigarron to himself. "There never was a wizard who died comfortably, in his bed. Already, I feel a rope about my throat. Ah me!"

At the end of the day, one of the King's pages came to bring him food. In despair, Juan Cigarron watched the jailer unlock the door for him to enter. He watched the page boy place the food on the bench before him and watched him turn away. All the time he was thinking: "Three days of life granted me—no more, no less—and already one is gone." As the jailer unlocked the door for the page to go out again, Juan Cigarron groaned:

"Ay, by San Bruno, this is no fun;
Of the three—there goes one!"

Hearing these words, the page took to his heels and ran as if the devil himself were after him. Finding the King's two other pages waiting for him in a corner of the palace wall, he told them quickly what Juan Cigarron had said.

"Not a doubt of it. He is the greatest wizard on earth. He knows we three have stolen the silver and buried it in the graveyard. We are undone. Let us go to him and confess."

"Never," said one of the others. "You are a weakling. Your ears did not hear right. Tomorrow I will carry his supper to him, and then we shall see."

At the end of the second day, Juan Cigarron's heart had become as heavy as the irons on his feet. With agony he watched the second page enter his dungeon, leave food, and depart. He groaned:

"Now, by San José, honest and true,
Of the three—I've counted two."

If one devil had been at the heels of the first page, a score were hounding the second. "He knows! He knows!" he screamed to the two boys waiting for him. "We are lost."

"Not yet," said the third and oldest page. "I myself will

carry his supper tomorrow night. I shall not run from the cell. I shall stand beside him and mark his words with care."

At the end of the third day, Juan Cigarron could feel a rope as if tied tightly about his neck. He could not eat his supper for choking. Looking up from his bench and seeing the third page still standing at his elbow, he thought, "Here is a lad who feels pity for me. . . ." And aloud he said:

"Good San Andrés, counsel me.
They've come and gone—all three!"

The page threw himself at the jailed feet of Juan Cigarron. He groveled there, shaking with fear.

"Master Wizard, pity us! Have compassion! Do not tell the King that it is his three pages who have stolen the silver. We will have our necks wrung tomorrow like so many cockerels if you do. Spare us and we will tell you where it lies buried. And never, never will we steal again."

With great dignity Juan Cigarron rose to his feet. "Do you not know that young rascals have a way of turning into old rascals? How do I know that by saving you now, I shall not be freeing you to commit more sins later? Enough groveling, now; I will pardon you this time. But you must swear by all the saints never to steal again—not so much as an *ochavito*. Tomorrow, when I appear before the King, you must in secret bring the silver to the dungeon here, every last piece of it."

So on the morrow Juan Cigarron was not hanged. He told the King where the silver plate would be found. And there it was, sure enough. The King was more than pleased. He embraced Juan Cigarron and kissed him on both cheeks.

"I did you a great wrong, and I shall make it up to you. From now on you shall be, not *a* wizard to all the world, but my own Royal Wizard. You shall live with me always, in the palace, where you will be handy to do a magic trick when the occasion arises. You are great—stupendous—more magnificent than all the wizards in the whole wide world!" He hugged Juan Cigarron again.

So Juan Cigarron lived in the palace, eating with the King, sleeping in a room next to his, and going where the King went.

But Juan Cigarron grew thinner and paler and unhappier every day. "What shall I do when the next trial comes! Ah me!" groaned Juan Cigarron, as each new hour in the day struck.

At last there came an evening when the King happened to be walking alone in his garden. He was smoking and thinking that it was time Juan Cigarron should have his wits and his magic put to the test again. Thinking he would play a clever trick on him, the King took his cigar from his mouth and pulled his wallet from his pocket. Into the wallet he stuffed the cigar, and then put them into his pocket. Next he sent a page to bring the wizard.

When Juan Cigarron stood before him, the King asked him, "What did I have in my mind that I took out of my mouth and put for safekeeping in my wallet?" He meant that he had been thinking of Cigarron, his wizard; he had been smoking *cigarron* and had put *cigarron* in his pocket.

Juan Cigarron was filled with terror. Here was doom descending upon him. Hardly knowing that he spoke, he muttered, more to himself than to the King:

"What a fool is man to pretend—
Poor Juan Cigarron has met a bad end!"

How the King laughed! He clapped his hand to his pocket, drew out his wallet, and showed the cigar snuffed out and quite dead. Casting it from him, he embraced Juan Cigarron for a third time and said: "That was as clever an answer as ever I heard. For that, I will grant any wish you wish to make."

"Any wish?" asked Juan Cigarron.

"Any wish," confirmed the King.

"Then I wish to end my days as a wizard tonight—and begin them tomorrow as a simple man."

Sweden

The Old Woman and the Tramp

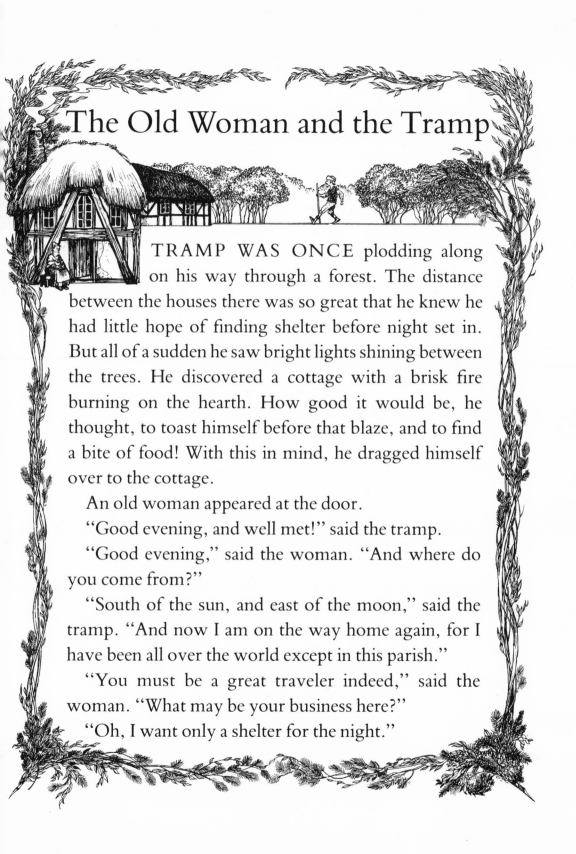

A TRAMP WAS ONCE plodding along on his way through a forest. The distance between the houses there was so great that he knew he had little hope of finding shelter before night set in. But all of a sudden he saw bright lights shining between the trees. He discovered a cottage with a brisk fire burning on the hearth. How good it would be, he thought, to toast himself before that blaze, and to find a bite of food! With this in mind, he dragged himself over to the cottage.

An old woman appeared at the door.

"Good evening, and well met!" said the tramp.

"Good evening," said the woman. "And where do you come from?"

"South of the sun, and east of the moon," said the tramp. "And now I am on the way home again, for I have been all over the world except in this parish."

"You must be a great traveler indeed," said the woman. "What may be your business here?"

"Oh, I want only a shelter for the night."

"I thought as much," said the woman. "But you may as well go away at once, for my husband is not at home and my cottage is not an inn."

"My good woman," said the tramp, "you must not be so hardhearted. We are both human beings. It is written that we should help one another."

"Help one another?" said the woman. "Help? Did you ever hear of such a thing? Who will help me, do you think? I haven't a morsel in the house! No, you must look for shelter elsewhere."

But the tramp was like the rest of his kind. He would not consider himself beaten at the first rebuff. Although the old woman grumbled, he kept at it. He begged like a starved dog, until at last she gave in and granted him permission to lie on the floor for the night.

That was very kind, he thought, and he thanked her for it.

"It is better to lie on the floor without sleep than to suffer cold in the forest deep," he said. He was a merry fellow, this tramp, and always ready with a rhyming word.

When he entered the cottage, he could see that the woman was not so badly off as she had pretended to be. She was just stingy and complaining.

The tramp tried to make himself agreeable as he asked her for something to eat.

"Where shall I get it?" asked the woman. "I haven't tasted a morsel the whole day."

But the tramp was a cunning fellow, he was.

"Poor old granny, you must be starving. Well, well, I suppose I shall have to ask you to have something with me, then."

"Have something with you!" said the woman. "You don't look as if you could ask anyone to have anything! What have you to offer, I should like to know?"

"He who far and wide does roam sees many things not known at home; and he who many things has seen has wits about him and senses keen," said the tramp, with more of his rhymes. "Better dead than to lose one's head! Lend me a pot, granny!"

The old woman had now grown curious, as you may guess. She let him have a big pot.

The tramp filled the pot with water and hung it over the fire. Then he blew and blew till the fire flared up brightly all around it. He took a four-inch nail from his pocket, carefully turned it around three times in his hand, and dropped it into the pot.

The woman stared. "What is this going to be?" she asked.

"Nail broth," said the tramp, and began to stir the water with the porridge whisk.

"Nail broth?" asked the woman.

"Yes, nail broth," said the tramp.

The old woman had seen and heard a good deal in her time, but that anybody could make broth with a nail, well, she had never heard the like of this before.

"That's something for poor people to know," she said, "and I should like to learn how to make it."

"That which is not worth having will always go a-begging," said the tramp.

But if she wanted to learn to make it, she had only to watch him, he said, and went on stirring the broth.

The old woman squatted near the hearth, her hands clasping her knees and her eyes following the tramp's hand as he stirred the broth.

"This generally makes good broth," he said; "but this time it will very likely be rather thin, for this whole week I have been making broth with the same nail. If only I had a handful of sifted meal to add, that would make it all right. But what one has to go without, it's no use thinking more about," and once again he stirred the broth.

"Well, I think I have a scrap of flour somewhere," said the old woman. She went to fetch it, and it was both good and fine.

The tramp began stirring the flour into the broth and went on stirring and stirring, while the woman sat, staring now at him and then at the pot, until her eyes seemed nearly to burst from their sockets.

"This broth would be good enough for company," the tramp now announced, putting in one handful of flour after another, "if only I had a bit of salted beef and a few potatoes to add. Indeed, it would be fit for gentlefolk, however particular they might be. But what one has to go without, it's no use thinking more about."

The old woman began to consider this, and she remembered she had a few potatoes, and perhaps there was a bit of beef as well. These she found and gave to the tramp, who went on stirring and stirring, while she sat and stared as hard as ever.

"This will be grand enough for the best in the land," he said at last.

"Well, I never!" said the woman. "And just fancy – all that with a nail!"

"If we had only a little barley and a drop of milk, we could ask the King himself to sup some of this. This is what he has every evening. That I know, for I have been in service under the King's cook," he said.

"Dear me! Ask the King to have some! Well, I never!" exclaimed the woman, slapping her knees. She was quite overcome by the tramp and his grand connections.

"But what one has to go without, it's no use thinking more about," said the tramp.

And then the woman remembered she had a little barley. And as for milk, well, she wasn't quite out of that, she said, for her best cow had just calved. She went to fetch both the one and the other.

The tramp went on with his stirring, and the woman with her staring, one moment at him and the next at the pot.

Suddenly the tramp took out the nail.

"Now it's ready, and we'll have a real feast. But with this kind of soup the King and the Queen always have something to drink, and one sandwich at least. And then they always have a cloth on the table when they eat," he added. "But what one has to go without, it's no use thinking more about."

By this time the old woman herself had begun to feel quite grand, I can tell you. If that was all that was wanted to make the soup just as the King had it, she thought it would be nice to have it just the same way for once, and play at being King and Queen with the tramp. So she went to a cupboard and brought out a bottle and glasses, butter and cheese, smoked beef and veal, until at last the table looked as if it were decked out for company.

Never in her life had the old woman eaten such a grand feast, and never had she tasted such broth. Just fancy, made only with a nail! She was in such a merry humor at having learned such an economical way of making broth that she

could not do enough for the tramp who had taught her such a useful thing.

The old woman and the tramp then ate and drank, and drank and ate, until their hunger was satisfied.

The tramp was ready to lie down on the floor to sleep. But that would never do, thought the old woman. No, that was impossible. Such a grand person must have a bed to lie in.

The tramp did not need much urging. "It's just like the sweet Christmas time. Happy are they who meet such good people." And he lay on the bed she offered him and went to sleep.

Next morning when the tramp awoke, the old woman was

ready with coffee for him. And as he was leaving, she gave him a bright dollar piece.

"And thanks, many thanks, for what you have taught me," she said. "Now I shall live in comfort, since I have learned how to make broth with a nail."

"Well, it isn't very difficult, if one only has something good to add to it," said the tramp as he went on his way.

The woman stood at the door staring after him.

"Such people don't grow on every bush," she said.

Lars, My Lad!

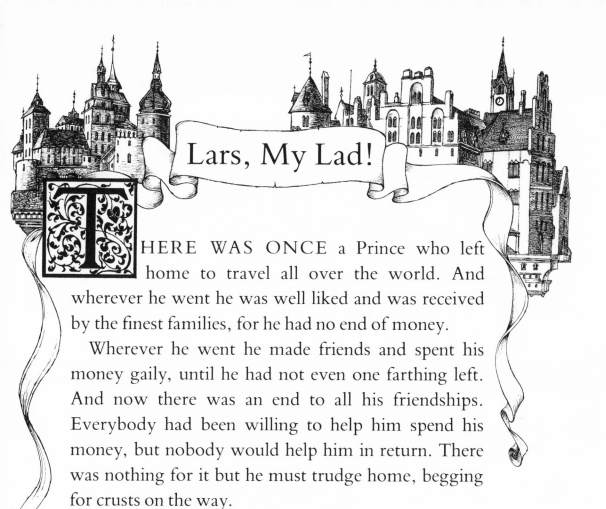

THERE WAS ONCE a Prince who left home to travel all over the world. And wherever he went he was well liked and was received by the finest families, for he had no end of money.

Wherever he went he made friends and spent his money gaily, until he had not even one farthing left. And now there was an end to all his friendships. Everybody had been willing to help him spend his money, but nobody would help him in return. There was nothing for it but he must trudge home, begging for crusts on the way.

Late one evening he came to a great forest. He kept on walking till he spied a tumbledown hut in the middle of a patch of bushes. It was not a suitable shelter for such a fine young man, but since there was no help for it, the Prince entered the hut. No one was to be seen. There was no stool to sit upon, but alongside one wall stood a big chest. What could there be in it? The Prince hoped he might find food there, for he had not eaten all day and was so hungry that his stomach groaned with pain. He lifted the lid.

Inside the chest was another chest, and in that another. And so it continued to be; in each chest was one smaller, until they became tiny boxes. The more he opened, the harder he worked at it. He felt there must be something valuable inside, to be so well hidden.

At last the Prince came to a miniature box in which lay a tiny piece of paper. That was all he found, for all his trouble! It disappointed him, but then he discovered something written on the paper. He was just able to make out the words *Lars, my lad!*

As he pronounced these words, he heard someone answer – right in his ear – "What are Master's orders?"

The Prince looked around, but he saw nobody. This was strange. He read out the words once more, "Lars, my lad!"

And the answer came as before, "What are Master's orders?"

He did not see anyone this time, either.

"If there is anybody about who hears what I say, then be kind enough to bring me something to eat," he asked.

The very next moment, there stood a table laid out with all the best things one could think of. The Prince ate and drank and thought he had never enjoyed himself so much in all his life.

When he had eaten all he could, he began to feel sleepy. He took out the paper again and said, "Lars, my lad!"

"What are Master's orders?" was the answer again.

"You have given me food and drink aplenty; now you must find me a bed to sleep in. But I want a really fine bed," he added. He was a bit more bold now that his hunger was satisfied.

Well, there it stood, a bed so fine that even the King himself might covet it.

This was all very well in its way, but when you become well off you wish for still more. No sooner had the Prince climbed into bed than he began to think that the room itself was altogether too poor for such a grand bed. Out came the paper again, and the words, "Lars, my lad!"

"What are Master's orders?" was the answer once more.

"Since you are able to supply me with such food and such a fine bed here in this forest, I am sure you can get me a better room. You see, I am accustomed to sleeping in a palace, with golden mirrors and covered walls, and ornaments and comforts of all kinds."

Well, no sooner had he spoken these words than he found himself lying in the most lavish chamber that anybody has ever seen.

Now, thought the Prince, he could be comfortable. He turned his face to the wall and closed his eyes to sleep, feeling quite satisfied.

But he had not yet seen all the grandeur. When he awoke and looked around in the morning, he saw that he had been sleeping in a great palace. He found that one room led into another, and wherever he turned he saw rich furnishings. The walls and ceilings glittered so with gold and silver that he had to shade his eyes when the sun shone on them.

Next he looked out of the windows. What grandeur out of doors, too! – not pine forests and juniper bushes any longer, but a garden with rare trees and roses of every kind.

Still the Prince could not see one human being, nor even a cat, and that made him lonely.

He took out the bit of paper and said again, "Lars, my lad!"

"What are Master's orders?" he heard again.

"Well, now that you have given me food and a bed, and a fine palace to live in, I intend to remain here, for I like the place. But I don't wish to live alone here. I must have both lads and lasses whom I may order about, to wait on me."

At once, there they were! – stewards and serving women, scullery maids and chambermaids. Some came bowing, some curtseying. Now the Prince thought he was satisfied.

But it happened that there was a large palace on the other side of the forest. As the King who owned it happened to look out of his window on waking, he saw the new palace. Golden weathercocks swung to and fro on its roof, dazzling his eyes.

"This is strange," he thought. He called his courtiers, who rushed in, bowing and scraping before him.

"Who is it that has dared to build such a palace on my land?" asked the King.

The courtiers bowed, and they scraped with their feet, but they did not know the answer.

The King then called his generals and captains. These came, stood at attention, and presented arms.

"Begone, soldiers," said the King, "and pull down that palace. Hang him who has built it, and don't lose any time about it!"

Well, they set off in haste to arm themselves, and away they

went. The drummers beat the skins of their drums, and the trumpeters blew their trumpets, and the other musicians played and blew as best they could, so that the Prince heard them long before he could see them. But he had heard that kind of noise before, and knew what it meant. He took out his scrap of paper and said, "Lars, my lad!"

"What are Master's orders?" he heard.

"There are soldiers coming here. You must provide me with soldiers and horses, that I may have double as many as those over in the wood. They must have sabers and pistols, and guns and cannon; but be quick about it."

No time was lost. When the Prince looked out, he beheld an immense number of soldiers drawn up around the palace.

When the King's men arrived, they came to a sudden halt and dared not advance nearer. The Prince was not afraid. He went straight to the officer in charge of the King's soldiers and asked him what he wanted.

The officer told him.

"It's of no use," said the Prince. "You can see how many men I have. If the King will listen to me, we can become good friends. I will be glad to help him against his enemies, and in such a way that this will be heard of far and wide."

The officer agreed with the Prince, and the Prince invited him and his men inside the palace, where he feasted them well.

While they were dining, they began to talk. The Prince thus learned that the King had a daughter, who was his only child. She was so wonderfully fair that no one had seen her like before. The more the soldiers ate and drank, the more they thought she would suit the Prince well for a wife.

They talked so long that the Prince began to be of the same opinion as the King's men. "But," said the soldiers, "she is as proud as she is beautiful. She will never look at a man."

The Prince only laughed at this. "If that is all, there is sure to be a remedy."

When the soldiers could eat no more, they set out homeward. Before they left, the Prince made sure to ask them to greet the King for him and say that he would call on him the next day.

When the Prince was alone again, he began to think of the Princess and to wonder if she could be as beautiful as the soldiers had said. He must make sure of it. So many strange things had happened that day; it might be possible to find that out, he thought.

"Lars, my lad!"

"What are Master's orders?"

"You must bring me the King's daughter as soon as she has gone to sleep, but she must not be awakened either on the way here or on the way back. Do you hear that?" he asked.

Before long the Princess was lying on a bed before him. She was sleeping soundly and looked exquisitely beautiful as she lay there.

The Prince walked all around her. He found her to be just as lovely from one side as from another.

The more he looked at her, the more he liked her.

"Lars, my lad!"

"What are Master's orders?"

"You must now carry the Princess home," he said, "for now I know how she looks, and tomorrow I will ask for her hand."

Next morning the King looked out of the window. "I suppose I shall not be troubled with the sight of that palace anymore," he thought. But, zounds! There it stood just as on the day before. With the sun shining brightly on its roof, the golden weathercocks dazzled his eyes again.

He became furious, and called his men.

More quickly than usual, in they came.

The courtiers bowed and scraped, and the soldiers stood at attention and presented arms.

"Do you see that palace?" screamed the King.

The courtiers and soldiers stared and gaped. Yes, of course, they saw it.

"Did I not order you to pull down the palace and hang the builder?" he cried.

They could not deny this, but they reported what had happened and how many soldiers the Prince had. Also they reported how the Prince had asked them to give his greetings to the King.

The King was confused. He had to put his crown on the table and scratch his head. Although he was a King, he could not understand this. He knew that the palace had been built in but a single night. It must have been magic that created it.

While the King was pondering this, the Princess came into the room.

"Good morning, Father. Just fancy, I had such a strange and beautiful dream last night!"

"What did you dream, my girl?" asked the King.

"I dreamed that I was in that new palace over yonder, and that I saw a Prince there so handsome that I could never have imagined his like. Now I want to get married, Father."

"You want to get married! You, who have never cared to look at a man! That's very strange!" said the King.

"That may be," said the Princess. "But it's different now. I want to get married, and it's that Prince I want."

The King was quite beside himself, so frightened was he of the Prince and his magic.

All of a sudden he heard a great sound of drums and trumpets. Then came a message that the Prince had arrived with a large company of followers, all so grandly dressed that gold and silver glistened in every fold of their garments. The King put on his crown and his fine coronation robes and went out on the palace steps to receive the Prince and his retinue. The Princess was not slow to follow her father.

The Prince bowed most graciously, and the King of course did the same. When they had discussed their affairs and their grandeur, they appeared to have become the best of friends. A great banquet was prepared and the Prince was seated next to the Princess. The Prince spoke so well for himself that the Princess could not say no to anything he said.

The Prince then went to the King and asked for the hand of the Princess. The King could not very well say no either, but before settling matters, he wanted to see the Prince's palace.

So it was arranged that the King should visit the Prince and take the Princess with him to see the new palace.

When the Prince returned home, Lars became busier than ever, for there was much to attend to. When the King and his daughter arrived, they found everything so magnificent that words could not describe it. The King appeared pleased.

The wedding was celebrated in grand style, and when the Prince arrived home with his bride, he, too, gave a great feast.

Time passed. One evening the Prince heard the words, "Are you satisfied now?"

It was Lars, as you may guess, but the Prince could not see him.

"Well, I ought to be," said the Prince. "You have provided me with everything."

"Yes, but what have I received in return?" asked Lars.

"Nothing," said the Prince, "but, bless me, what could I have given you, who are not of flesh and blood, and whom I cannot see? If there is anything I can do for you, tell me what it is, and I shall do it."

"Well, I should like that little scrap of paper that you found in the chest," said Lars.

"Nothing else?" said the Prince. "If such a trifle can help you, I can easily do without it, for now I know the words by heart."

Lars thanked the Prince, and asked him to put the paper on the chair in front of his bed when he retired. He would get it during the night.

The Prince did as he was told, then he and the Princess went to sleep.

Early in the morning the Prince awoke, so cold that his teeth chattered. When he opened his eyes, he found he had not a stitch on his back. Instead of lying on a grand bed in a beautiful bedroom within a magnificent palace, he lay on the big chest in the old hut.

The Prince began to shout, "Lars, my lad!" but he got no answer. He shouted once more, "Lars, my lad!" but got no answer this time either. So he shouted as loud as he could, "*Lars, my lad!*" It was all in vain.

Now the Prince began to understand. When Lars had the scrap of paper, he became freed from service, and he had taken everything with him.

There was no help for it. The Princess had only her clothes. She had got them from her father, and Lars had no power over them.

The Prince had to tell the Princess how everything had happened, and he asked her to leave him. He would have to manage as best as he could, he said. But the Princess would not hear of it. She remembered well what the parson had said when he married them. She would never, never leave her husband.

In the meantime, the King in his palace had also awakened, and when he looked out of his window, he did not see the Prince's palace. He became uneasy, and he called his courtiers.

The courtiers trooped in and began to bow and scrape.

"Do you see the palace over yonder behind the forest?" asked the King.

The men stared with all their might.

No, they did not see it.

"Where has it gone to, then?" asked the King.

Well, really they did not know.

It was not long before the King was on his way with his court. When they arrived where the palace should have been, they could see nothing but heather and juniper bushes. But among the bushes the King discovered the old hut. He entered and found his son-in-law, and his daughter weeping and moaning.

"Dear, dear! What does all this mean?" asked the King. But he did not get an answer, for the Prince could not bring himself to tell the King what had happened.

In spite of the King's promises and threats, the Prince remained silent.

The King became angry, for he could see that this Prince was not what he pretended to be. He ordered the Prince to be hanged, and at once. The Princess begged that mercy be shown the Prince, but neither her prayers nor her tears were of any help. An impostor should be hanged, said the King.

So it was to be.

The Prince had time to reflect on how foolish he had been in not saving some of the crumbs when he was living in plenty. And how stupid he had been in letting Lars have the scrap of paper. If only he had it again! They should see that he had gained some sense in return for all he had lost.

Just before the sun set in the forest, the Prince heard a great shouting. When he looked, he saw seven cartloads of worn-out shoes, and on top of the hindmost cart he spied a little old man in gray with a red pointed cap on his head. His face was like that of a poor scarecrow, and the rest of him not handsome either.

Straight he drove to the gallows where the Prince was awaiting his end. He looked at the Prince, and burst out laughing.

"How stupid you were! What should a fool do with his stupidity if he did not make use of it?" Then he laughed again. "Yes, there you are, and here am I carting away all the shoes I have worn out for your whims. I wonder if you can read what is written on this bit of paper, and if you recognize it?" With an ugly laugh, he held up the paper before the Prince's eyes.

This time it was Lars who was the fool, for the Prince,

although he had a rope about his neck, snatched the paper from him.

"Lars, my lad!"

"What are Master's orders?"

"You must cut this rope and put the palace and all the rest in place again, exactly as before. And when night has come, you must bring back the Princess."

All went merrily as in a dance, and before long everything was in its place.

When the King awoke the next morning, he looked out of the window as usual. There stood the palace again with its weathercocks glittering beautifully in the sunshine. He called his courtiers at once.

"Do you see the palace over there?" asked the King.

Yes, of course they did.

The King sent for the Princess, but she was not to be found. He went out to see if his son-in-law was hanging, but neither son-in-law nor gallows were to be seen.

At once the King set off through the forest. When he came to the place where the palace should stand, there it stood, sure enough. The gardens and the roses were exactly as they used to be, and the Prince's attendants. The Prince and the Princess, dressed in their finest, received the King.

"Well, I never saw the like of this," said the King to himself. He could not believe his eyes.

"God's peace be with you, Father, and welcome here!" said the Prince.

The King stared at him.

"Are you my son-in-law?" he asked.

"Well, I suppose I am," said the Prince. "Who else could I be?"

"Did I not order you to be hanged yesterday like any common thief?" asked the King.

"I think you must have been bewitched on the way," said the Prince with a laugh. "Do you think I am the man to allow myself to be hanged? Or does anyone here dare to believe it? If anyone dares to say the King could have wished me such evil, let him speak," said the Prince.

How could anyone dare to say such a thing? No, they hoped they had more sense than that.

The King did not know what to believe, for when he looked at the Prince he thought he could never have wished him evil. But still he was not quite convinced.

"Did I not come here yesterday, and was not the whole palace gone, and was there not an old hut standing in its place? And did I not go into that hut and see you there?"

"I wonder that the King can talk so," said the Prince. "I think the trolls must have bewitched your eyes and made you crazy. Or what do *you* think?" he said, and turned around to the King's courtiers.

These all bowed till their backs were bent double, and agreed with everything he said. The King rubbed his eyes and looked around him.

"I suppose it is as you say, then," he said to the Prince. "It is well I have got back my proper sight and have come to my senses again, for it would have been a shame to have let you be hanged." He was happy again, and nobody thought any more about the matter.

The Prince now took it upon himself to manage his affairs, so that it was seldom Lars had to wear down his shoes. The King soon gave the Prince half of his kingdom, so he had plenty to do. People began to say that they would have to search a long time to find his equal in wisdom and justice.

One day Lars came to the Prince, looking very little better than before. But this time he was more humble, and did not dare to giggle and make faces.

"You do not want my help any longer," he said. "But I used to wear out my shoes, now I am unable to do so. My feet will soon be covered with moss. Now perhaps you might let me go."

The Prince agreed. "I have tried to spare you, and I almost think I could do without you. But the palace and all the rest I do not want to lose, for such a clever builder as you I shall never get again. I cannot give you back the paper on any account."

"Well," said Lars, "as long as you have it, I need not fear; but if anybody else should get it, there would be nothing but running about again, and that's what I want to avoid. When one has been tramping about as I have done, one begins to tire of it."

At last they agreed that the Prince should put the paper

in the box and bury it twenty feet under the ground, beneath a stone. They then thanked one another and parted.

The Prince carried out his part of the agreement, which he was not likely to want to change. He and the Princess lived happily and had both sons and daughters. When the King died, the Prince inherited the whole of the kingdom, and he reigns there still, if he is not dead.

As for that box with the scrap of paper in it, there are many who are still running about looking for it.

FINIS

The stories in this collection were adapted and retold from the following sources:

THE WOOD FAIRY is retold from a literal translation by Halina Berovetz of the story told by Bozena Nemcova in *Babička* (Praha, Státní nakl. dětské knihy, 1951) and from the translation by W. W. Strickland of the version by Karel Erben in *Panslavonic Folklore* (New York, B. Westermann, 1930).

THE TWELVE MONTHS is retold from *Fairy Tales of the Slav Peasants and Herdsmen*, from the French of Aleksandr Borejko Chodzko; trans. and illus. by Emily J. Harding (London, George Allen, 1896).

EE-AW! EE-AW! is retold with some adaptation from *Fairy Tales from Afar.* Translated from the Danish of Svend Herbert Grundtvig by Jane Mulley. New York, A. Wessels Company, 1902.

THE WONDERFUL POT is retold with some adaptation from *Danish Fairy and Folk Tales, A Collection of Popular Stories and Fairy Tales.* Translated by J. Christian Bay from the Danish of Svend Grundtvig, E. T. Kristensen, Ingvor Bondesen, and L. Budde. New York and London, Harper, 1899.

JACK AND THE BEANSTALK, TOM THUMB, and DICK WHITTINGTON AND HIS CAT have been retold from *English Fairy Tales* collected by Joseph Jacobs (originally published 1892 by G. P. Putnam's Sons).

PUSS IN BOOTS and THE SLEEPING BEAUTY IN THE WOOD, from *Histoires ou Contes du Temps Passé* by Charles Perrault (1697).

THE TWELVE DANCING PRINCESSES, from *Contes du Roi Cambrinus* by Charles Deulin (Paris, E. Dentu, Editeur, Libraire de la Société des Gens de Lettres, 1874).

RUMPELSTILTSKIN, HANSEL AND GRETEL, and THE BREMEN TOWN MUSICIANS, from the folklore collected in Germany by Jakob and Wilhelm Grimm, have been translated and retold from their *Kinder und Hausmärchen* (originally published 1812–24).

CONSTANTES AND THE DRAGON is retold from E. M. Geldart's *Folklore of Modern Greece: The Tales of the People.* London, S. Swan Sonnenschein and Company, 1884.

THE FAIRY WIFE is retold from *Fairy Tales of Modern Greece,* by Theodore P. Gianakoulis & Georgia H. MacPherson. Dutton, 1930.

THE BLIND MAN, THE DEAF MAN, AND THE DONKEY and THE VALIANT CHATTEE-MAKER are retold from *Old Deacon Days; or, Hindoo Fairy Legends Current in Southern India,* collected in India by Mary E. Frere (Philadelphia, Lippincott, 1868).

THE BEE, THE HARP, THE MOUSE AND THE BUM-CLOCK, from *Donegal Fairy Stories* by Seumas MacManus (Garden City, New York: Doubleday, Page and Company, 1899). By permission of Patricia MacManus.

BILLY BEG AND THE BULL, from *In Chimney Corners,* by Seumas MacManus (Garden City, New York: Doubleday, Page and Company, 1899). By permission of Patricia MacManus.

CENERENTOLA is retold from Giambattista Basile's *Stories from the Pentamerone,* selected and edited by E. F. Strange (London, Macmillan, 1911), which follows the translation by John Edward Taylor, 1847. CENERENTOLA is a Neapolitan tale.

BASTIANELO is retold from Thomas F. Crane's *Italian Popular Tales* (Boston, Houghton Mifflin Company, 1885). BASTIANELO is a Venetian tale collected by Dom Guiseppe Bernoni in his *Fiabe Populari Veneziani,* 1873.

THE TONGUE-CUT SPARROW and THE WHITE HARE AND THE CROCODILES are retold from *Japanese Fairy Tales,* compiled by Yei Theodora Ozaki (Tokyo, 1904; New York, A. L. Burt, 1905). The preface to this volume states that "this collection of Japanese folk tales is the outcome of a suggestion made to me indirectly through a friend by Mr. Andrew Lang. They have been translated from the modern version written by Sadanami Sanjin. These stories are not literal translations, and though the Japanese story and all the quaint Japanese expressions have been faithfully preserved, they have been told more with the view to interest young readers of the West than the technical student of folk-lore. . . . In one or two instances I have gathered an incident from another version."

WHY THE SEA IS SALT and THE THREE BILLY GOATS GRUFF, adapted from the 1859 translation by Sir George Webb Dasent of Norwegian folk tales gathered by Peter Christian Asbjornsen and Jorgen E. Moe.

ABOUT THE HEDGEHOG WHO BECAME PRINCE, from *Polish Fairy Book* by Elsie Byrde (New York, Stokes, 1927).

THE JOLLY TAILOR WHO BECAME KING, from *The Jolly Tailor and Other Fairy Tales Translated from the Polish,* by Lucia Borski (Copyright 1928 and renewed 1956, by Longmans, Green and Company, Inc., New York).

SNEGOURKA, THE SNOW MAIDEN, from *Folk-Lore and Legends, Russian and Polish,* edited by "C.S.P." (London, Gibbings, 1890; Philadelphia, J. B. Lippincott Company, 1891).

THE FLYING SHIP, from RUSSIAN FAIRY TALES, selected and translated from *The Skazki of Polevoi,* by R. Nisbet Bain (London, Lawrence and Bullen, 1892).

THE PAGE BOY AND THE SILVER GOBLET, THE BROWNIE O' FERNE-DEN, from *Scottish Fairy Tales* by Elizabeth W. Grierson (New York, Stokes, 1910).

FOUR BROTHERS WHO WERE BOTH WISE AND FOOLISH, by Ruth Sawyer, copyright 1946 by Story Parade, Inc. Reprinted by permission of David Durand.

JUAN CIGARRON, by Ruth Sawyer, copyright 1941 by Story Parade, Inc. Reprinted by permission of David Durand.

THE OLD WOMAN AND THE TRAMP and LARS, MY LAD! are retold from *Fairy Tales from the Swedish* by Nils Gabriel Djurklou (New York, F. A. Stokes Co., 1901), translated by H. L. Braekstad.

865

DECATUR PUBLIC LIBRARY
3 1202 00511 2136

12/97 11/7/97 -52

GAYLORD R